baby love

baby love

Healthy, Easy, Delicious Meals for Your Baby and Toddler

Norah O'Donnell and Chef Geoff Tracy

 St. Martin's Griffin ⚑ New York

www.stmartins.com

Book design and composition by Gretchen Achilles/Wavetrap Design

Photography by Timothy Devine

Library of Congress Cataloging-in-Publication Data

O'Donnell, Norah.
    Baby love : healthy, easy, delicious meals for your baby and ιddler / Norah
O'Donnell and Geoff Tracy.—1st ed.
       p. cm.
    ISBN 978-0-312-62192-6
1. Cookery (Baby foods) 2. Natural foods. 3. Infants—Nutrition. I. Tracy, Geoff. II.
Title.
    TX740.O423 2010
    641.5'6222—dc22   2010010094

First Edition: August 2010

10   9   8   7   6   5   4   3   2   1

To Grace, Henry, and Riley . . . We love you.

contents

the way to a baby's heart

Our lives are very, very busy. Geoff is a trained chef and has five restaurants. I am a television anchor and correspondent who covers politics with NBC. Geoff and I don't work full time, we work all the time. We also have three beautiful young children. Grace and Henry are twins. Riley was born thirteen months later. Seriously, we had three kids in thirteen months! They make work seem like a piece of cake.

grace o'donnell tracy—age 2

(1 MINUTE OLDER THAN HENRY) Without question, Grace is the most dominant person in the family. She overflows with passion and energy and takes after her Granny Franny. When the teacher forms a circle of kids, Grace thinks that is her sign to get in the middle. She is compassionate and is sincerely interested in the feelings of everyone in the room. She loves to "big jump" off just about anything and always has skinned knees and bruises from playing at the park. A good eater, she enjoys yogurt, pancakes, and bubbly water. Her favorite colors are purple and pink. She actually believes that everything in the world that is pink . . . is hers.

henry o'donnell tracy—age 2

(1 MINUTE YOUNGER THAN GRACE) "Hank the Tank" was born smaller than his twin sister. As a newborn he had a furrowed brow that made him appear more serious than any baby should. He has the most beautiful red hair and has grown into a very handsome and strong boy. He was the first to figure out how to open a door and knows how to use the key to start the ignition in the minivan. These days, he loves guitars, watering flowers, scooters, vacuums, and hunting acorns. Henry's favorite color is blue because Grace told him so. His favorite foods are bananas and raisins although recently he has developed a regular hankering for fresh pasta and marinara from "Daddy's restaurant."

riley norah tracy—age 1

(13 MONTHS YOUNGER THAN THE TWINS)

Fondly known to the twins as "Giant Baby," Riley is just an inch smaller than them. She's 99th percentile on height and, like the twins, very lean. She is so tall for her age that people think we have triplets. Riley was a perfect baby and slept through the night from the start. She eats everything. Currently her favorite foods are Alba's Chicken Soup, strawberries, and "arbolitos" (that's Spanish for "little trees," which is broccoli). Riley loves chasing the cat, swimming lessons, and cuddling. She loves rock 'n' roll and will jam to the music. She also giggles anytime she gets to wrestle with the twins. Her favorite color is green.

Even with demanding jobs and hectic schedules, our children remain our number-one priority. Nothing is more precious to us than their smiles, their happiness, and *their health*. When we became parents we decided to make sure that we were never too busy to provide wholesome, nutritious food for our children. The food that is lovingly spoon-fed to a six-month-old child is the first food other than breast milk or formula. It is the cornerstone of a lifelong healthy relationship with food. It is quite literally the *way to a baby's heart*.

Like busy parents everywhere we figured out how to make it work, and we want to share that with you.

Here's the secret: making fresh baby food is pretty simple stuff. In fact, it is really easy and can take less than an hour every two weeks to prepare. Our recipes are fast and easy, delicious and super inexpensive. Plus, there's no better way to build a foundation for a lifetime of healthy living.

And this is important. One in three children in America is now at risk of being overweight or obese. Bad eating habits are learned early. It starts with infants and toddlers and the fast-food instinct of feeding from a jar or can.

So our mission is simple: we want to help people understand the importance and benefits of fresh, nutritious baby food and ignite a homemade baby-food craze across the country. In the past few years, America has experienced a great food awakening. Thanks to the slow-food and farm-to-table movements, food-conscious adults have moved away from overprocessed imported "Frankenfood," and embraced the benefits of natural, organic, local food. Thus far, our babies have too often been left out of this dining trend. We believe the time is ripe for change and look forward to a great baby food revolution.

So, why *Baby Love*?

It's easy! You can make two weeks' worth of wholesome food in less than one hour a week! This is really simple stuff with simple recipes to follow. Once you've pureed the fresh natural ingredients,

pour them into ice cube trays and freeze. The next day, pop them out and store them in zipper bags. When it comes time for a meal, warm up two or three cubes in a pan or microwave, strap on the bib, and it's time for some baby love.

It's delicious! Have you ever tasted a jar of canned baby pea puree? Yucky! Now, have you ever tasted fresh pureed peas? They're so delicious you could use the puree as a soup at a dinner party. (Just add a little pat of butter and some salt!)

It's inexpensive! Making fresh baby food is less expensive than mass produced food, in some cases as much as 80 percent cheaper. A diet of *Baby Love* Chicken Soup, Perfectly Basic Carrot, and Perfectly Basic Apple for six months would cost about $260. Store-bought jarred foods would cost about $650 for the same amount. The cost savings are dramatic. And by making your own food, there is less packaging, less waste, and thus it's better for the environment.

It's nutritious! Nothing beats fresh fruits, vegetables, and meats. The ingredients of some jarred foods include modified cornstarch. Plus, in order to maintain a longer shelf life, the foods are cooked at such a high temperature that many of the nutrients and flavors are lost.

1.
introducing baby love

getting started

Babies are ready to begin eating solid foods at four to six months of age. At this time almost all babies can learn to eat from a spoon. Most start with rice cereal mixed with breast milk or formula.

If all is going well, check with your pediatrician about beginning to feed your munchkin simple pureed fruits or vegetables. Some pediatricians recommend you start with vegetables first to avoid developing a sweet tooth. However, the American Academy of Pediatrics states that "there is no evidence that your baby will develop a dislike for vegetables if fruit is given first. Babies are born with a preference for sweets, and the order of introducing foods does not change this."

New foods should be introduced one at a time. Wait at least two to three days before starting another to make sure your child is not allergic. Watch for any allergic reactions such as diarrhea, rash, or vomiting. Once, our son, Henry, broke out in a facial rash. We called the doctor, who suggested it might be the tomatoes in the Bolognese! Sometimes infants don't like the acidity in tomatoes. The lesson: stop the food and then check with your doctor about the reaction.

We also made the decision to introduce new foods at breakfast or lunchtime rather than at dinnertime. In case the twins got a tummyache or gas at least it was during the day. You don't want a gassy baby keeping you up all night!

Within a few months of starting purees, your baby should be enjoying all sorts of fruits, vegetables, and meats. You know the saying, "Variety is the spice of life!" There is no better time to introduce these healthy foods.

your baby's stages

FIRST TASTES: 6 MONTHS AND UP

START SIMPLE

Watching your baby grow up and change and experience new things is one of the great joys of parenting. It's so exciting when your infant is ready for one of the big milestones in life: starting solids. It's also a good time to get out the camera and take pictures, as they usually enjoy smearing the food all over their faces!

Pediatricians recommend you start simple. First up is the baby cereal. Rice cereal is often recommended because it is gluten-free and is not likely to cause an allergic reaction. Also, commercially produced rice cereal is iron-fortified, an important nutrient for your baby's physical and mental development.

You'll notice babies only like a couple of tiny spoonfuls of the baby rice cereal mixed with breast milk or formula. Slowly, they will begin to take more and more and will eat a small bowl. We learned that feeding the cereal to Henry and Grace before bedtime actually helped them sleep longer at night!

Next, we started mashing banana and mixing it in with the cereal. Bananas are truly one of the world's super foods: they are not only nutritious but can help babies with constipation and diarrhea. More on the health benefits of bananas later!

Signs your baby is ready for solid food:

- Head control: Baby can hold head upright

- Sitting up: Baby can sit in high chair

- Smacking lips: Baby moves mouth while watching others eat; expresses interest in eating food

- Tongue-thrust: Baby stops pushing food out of the mouth (sometimes called the tongue-thrusting reflex)

Finally, during this stage you can begin *Baby Love*'s "Perfectly Basic" single-ingredient recipes of apple, pear, banana, avocado, pea, carrot, butternut squash, and sweet potato.

Sometimes when we were in a pinch for time, we'd just use a fork to mash up some banana and avocado together. There's no cooking at all! The sweet taste of the banana really helps make the avocado palatable for your wee one. My friend and mother of three, Emily, recommends adding a couple drips of orange juice just to help smooth out the texture. Delicious! Remember, introduce each food one at a time and wait two to three days to check for any allergic reaction.

During this time, your baby may begin eating

three small meals a day. That is approximately 4 ounces or two ice cubes each meal. And that's just a guideline. We learned from our twins that some days they are really hungry—and other days, not so

The American Academy of Pediatrics says because many adult foods contain added salt and preservatives, they should not be fed to babies.

much. Plus they go through these growth spurts and you will notice they seem like they just keep eating and never stop!

FUN WITH FLAVOR: 8 MONTHS AND UP

START MIXING IT UP!
By now, your baby may be crawling around and starting to stick everything in her mouth. Our daughter Riley was already teething at this point and clearly seemed ready for the next stage early. She was developmentally ahead of the twins at this age. And that's perfectly normal. It's also why pediatricians recommend you follow your baby's cues. Some infants will be ready before others to advance to the next food stage. In this stage, it's about mixing ingredients and adding herbs and spices, perhaps some dairy or proteins.

Your baby will still eat many of the purees she started at six months. But now you can work in Cinnamon Apple Oatmeal Raisin, a delicious recipe that makes your house smell like heaven after you've cooked it!

Our doctor also advised us that it was time to introduce proteins and foods with additional sources of iron that are absolutely crucial to healthy brain development. A baby is born with a store of iron that lasts about six months. So it's imperative, say nutritionists, to include iron-rich foods like meat, fish, and poultry.

Our nanny, Alba, came up with a perfect chicken

introducing baby love • 5

soup recipe—a delicious combination of protein, vegetables, and rice. It's a real super-food recipe and truly our children's favorite meal. We have to admit each of our three kids ate it practically every day as babies because it was just packed with so many wholesome ingredients! Plus, Alba always left me a bowl of chicken soup to eat when I got home from work. What a treat!

TOTS LOVE TEXTURE: 10 MONTHS AND UP
FINGER FOODS!

At this stage, your baby is still enjoying purees and is ready to start slowly adding some foods with texture.

Your infant may be trying to walk. He may also have teeth and can use a pincer grasp to put finger foods in between his thumb and forefinger. So now is the time to introduce some soft combination foods along with the purees they still need. You can start the zucchini or butternut risottos, orzo with cheese (aka mac 'n' cheese), or small diced up whole grain pancakes.

You can also cut up small pieces of banana, avocado, mango, and other fruits.

GETTING BIG: 12 MONTHS AND UP
Happy birthday! The one-year birthday is a big milestone. Your infant is now likely to be walking and starting to say a few words.

The first big thing about the twelve-month mark is the transition to whole milk. Don't give your baby reduced-fat milk. The American Academy of Pediatrics is pretty clear about this. A baby needs the fat calories that whole milk offers for healthy development. Up until age two, fats should make up half of the daily intake of calories. In fact, you should not consider lower-fat milk an option until after your child's second birthday.

I recommend making the transition to whole milk gradually. For instance, Riley was drinking 8 ounces of formula per bottle. I started mixing 2 ounces of organic whole milk in with 6 ounces of the formula. You may notice some loose stools at first. A week later, I did 4 ounces milk mixed with 4 ounces formula. You get the idea.

Changes in poop! Don't freak out if you notice your baby's poop is starting to change color and stink even more after you introduce solid foods. Vegetables can produce an amazing variety of poop colors. It is not unusual to open the diaper and discover yellow, green, or even red bowel movements. As always, check with your pediatrician if you are concerned.

it's nutritious

When we first decided to make our children homemade purees our main rationale was that it's healthy, easy, and delicious. It just seemed like the right thing to do. But the more and more I read and learn about nutrition, the more I am convinced that it is absolutely crucial to their lifelong health and happiness. Make no mistake: what you feed your baby now will affect the rest of their lives.

Did you know that children grow more rapidly in the first year than at any other time in their lifetime? Did you know that much of a human's brain growth occurs in the first few years of life? In fact, there is so much rapid growth and cell division in the body that scientists believe infancy and the toddler years are the best window of opportunity to influence adult health. It's called "metabolic programming," the idea that the foods eaten in childhood can have long-lasting—even permanent—effects on how the body grows and functions and wards off disease.

I am indebted to Dr. Susan B. Roberts, Ph.D., who coauthored the book *Feeding Your Child for Lifelong Health* and is also the author of *The Instinct Diet* for parents. She really opened my eyes to the powerful effects of early choices. Dr. Roberts points out that during the early years, as all these cells throughout the body are growing, they are sensitive to the availability of nutrients. "The nutrients present at this crucial time of cell division and growth help determine which cell types become predominant with each tissue," she says. These tissues and organs become important in the essential body processes of hormone production and enzyme activity. So you can see why the programming of these cells begins so early.

Dr. Roberts notes that "metabolic programming gives your child's body directions for his future. We know that first foods can have permanent effects on growth, strength, the immune system, and intelligence—with long-term consequences for many other aspects of health and even personality. Through metabolic programming, our children's whole lives are influenced by what they eat in their early years."

Good early habits can help prevent obesity, avoid allergies, optimize bone strength and height, maybe boost intelligence, and prevent childhood and adult cancers.

The other important reason for making homemade purees is that good eating habits are learned early. Babies who eat fresh fruits and vegetables grow up to be children who eat nutritiously. It's a wonder to watch our daughter Riley eat steamed broccoli pieces like they are chocolate-covered strawberries. The nutrition experts say that from nine to eighteen months we are given this incredible opportunity to put just about anything healthy on our child's plate and train their taste buds to enjoy wholesome foods forever.

So, bottom line: healthy eating in infancy is quite simply the cornerstone of a longer, healthier, and happier life.

FOODS TO AVOID

Babies can enjoy a wide variety of fruits, vegetables, meats, herbs, and spices. But there are some foods worth avoiding for health reasons, like allergies, risk of infection, or choking hazards.

ALLERGENIC FOODS

- Cow's milk

- Egg whites

- Soy

- Peanuts

- Tree nuts

- Wheat

- Tuna, mackerel, shark, swordfish

- Shellfish

First, if your family has a history with allergies check with your pediatrician about foods to avoid. When you do introduce solid foods to babies you should be aware that an overwhelming majority of the reactions are caused by milk, egg whites, soy, peanuts, tree nuts, wheat, and shellfish.

The American Academy of Pediatrics does not recommend introducing cow's milk until after one year of age because a baby can have trouble digesting the proteins. Cow's milk also does not have the complete nutrients a baby needs for growth.

The American Academy of Pediatrics recommends that because eggs are frequently associated with allergy, egg whites should not be introduced until after one year of age.

Fish like tuna, mackerel, shark, and swordfish have high mercury content and are not recommended. Your doctor probably already warned you against eating these types of fish during pregnancy.

CHOKING HAZARDS

- Grapes
- Cherry tomatoes
- Nuts
- Chips
- Popcorn
- Raisins

Anything not pureed should be cut up into pea-sized pieces to prevent choking or gagging. Vegetables should be cooked until soft and then cut into manageable pieces. Fruits like grapes or cherry tomatoes should be sliced into quarters.

INFECTION RISKS

- Honey
- Soft cheeses

Honey is an absolute no-no. It can contain bacteria spores that cause botulism, an illness that can be fatal. A child's intestinal tract is not mature enough to fight these life-threatening toxins. The American Academy of Pediatrics recommends that honey not be given to infants younger than twelve months.

Soft or unpasteurized cheeses can contain listeria, which can cause food poisoning.

SIMPLY NOT GOOD FOR BABIES

- Salt
- Sugar
- Spicy foods
- Fruit juices
- Hot dogs
- Deli meats

Babies are delicate and that's why some things should just be avoided. Salt can strain an infant's immature kidneys. Deli meats should also be avoided; they are often full of sodium and sometimes preservatives. Sugar is just not necessary and can cause tooth decay. Spicy foods are probably not worth it. Grace, at eighteen months, developed an affinity for hot salsa with her father's encouragement. I think she just likes the chips. Hot dogs, ham, bacon, and sausages are full of nitrates. The body can convert nitrates into potent carcinogens, which increase DNA damage and can lead to cancer.

Finally, pediatricians generally recommend not introducing fruit juices as a beverage to children at all, as they are high in sugar and just fill them up before meal time. Water is best. I made the mistake of giving my twins juice, but then learned to only offer Riley water for refreshment from the get-go. The twins still demand juice, so I usually fill the glass with half water and half juice. If you decide to introduce juice, the American Academy of Pediatrics suggests diluting it half and half with water and limit servings to no more than 4 ounces (½ cup). Only use 100 percent fruit juice, with no added sugars or other sweeteners.

The American Academy of Pediatrics also points out that fruit juices should not be introduced before six months of age. "Because of the non-absorbed carbohydrates in juices, large amounts of fruit juice can increase the frequency of stools and make them looser." This is also a reminder that if your little one is sick with diarrhea, you should avoid apple juice. Loose stools mean diaper rash, red bottoms, and very unhappy babies. Plus—they simply don't need the juice!

cheap cheap . . . and green!

Baby Love recipes are less expensive than store-bought baby foods. If you compare them to mass-produced jar baby food, high-end organic jar food, and the new extraordinarily expensive frozen baby foods now appearing in markets, you'll be amazed at how much money you will save. Some of this new store-bought stuff is 45 cents an ounce! That's more than $7 per pound! Imagine paying $7 a pound for pureed carrots and filtered water!

Below are some price comparisons between homemade and store-bought foods at a national chain.*

Baby Love Perfectly Basic Apple	$.11 per ounce
Baby Love Perfectly Basic Carrot	$.07 per ounce
Baby Love Perfectly Basic Pea	$.08 per ounce
Baby Love Alba's Chicken Soup	$.06 per ounce
Earth's Best Organic Baby Food (assorted)	$.20 per ounce
Gerber 2nd Foods Fruits (assorted)	$.18 per ounce
Gerber Meats (assorted) depending on pack size	$.15–.38 per ounce

A diet of *Baby Love* Alba's Chicken Soup, and Perfectly Basic Carrot and Apple for six months would cost about $260. A similar diet of mass-produced baby food would cost about $650!

We want to stress that this is not a book about penny pinching . . . but it doesn't hurt to have $390 extra in your pocket!

Baby Love is pretty green, too! It is amazing how much more garbage our family began producing once we had the twins. I had to order extra garbage and recycling bins from the city. Stinky diapers, wipes, formula containers, gifts, toys, cardboard . . . it all fills up those bins so fast. If your baby eats the mass-produced mush at the rate of three jars of baby food per day, you'll be recycling 540 glass jars before he or she reaches his or her first birthday.

*All prices sourced from safeway.com, September 2009

2.

words from chef geoff

My earliest memories are of food. Frozen crinkle cut French fries baking in the oven with their jagged cut and slightly burnt smell. Although I was only two years old, I can still recall the bag coming out of the green-colored freezer and the taste of hot puffy potato combined with very cold ketchup snatched from the refrigerator. The fries were always unevenly cooked.

As a young eater, I survived on cheese, crackers, raisins, peanuts, and raw carrot sticks. I was completely removed from the cooking and preparation of what I ate. And to a large extent so were my parents. Until I was ten, I thought vegetables came from a freezer. I had no idea they grew from soil and trees. Every green vegetable in our house was overcooked. One summer night, at a patio table behind our house, I declared brussels sprouts to be the worst vegetable in the world. I renamed them "killer vegetables."

When I was thirteen I started to experiment and enjoy food. I remember a farmer's market in New England where we bought fresh tomatoes, lettuce, and corn. That dusty sweet flavor of the tomato vine is still one of my favorite smells in the world. The corn was just picked and it was utterly delicious. My view of vegetables began to change and the world of food opened up to me. As an adult, I graduated first in my class from the Culinary Institute of America, the most prestigious culinary school in the world. Two years after graduating I opened my first restaurant at age twenty-seven. Nine years later, I was running five.

When I became a dad, it never once crossed my mind to feed my children mass-produced baby mush. I knew I didn't want my kids to wait until their teens to truly discover good food. I want them to be connected to their food from the start. I want them to understand that it comes from the earth and to see it prepared and cooked in their own home. I actually like brussels sprouts now! They just have to be fresh and cooked correctly.

Making baby food for my children was also an expression of love. As a dad, you are limited in your ability to provide sustenance during a pregnancy and the first half year of your child's life. But at six months I could play a role. It became a bonding experience with my babies and something that will always be an important and memorable part of my relationship with all three of them.

I spoke to another dad one afternoon at the playground and the topic of baby food came up. He was mortified at the stuff he was feeding his child. The color, the smell, and the appearance of it were all awful. He wouldn't even taste it himself. And yet, he fed it to his child. The reality is that many parents feel the same way. They use the mass-produced stuff because it was what they were fed as babies;

they don't think they have the time to make it themselves; they don't think they can cook for a baby—or at all.

As a result, most kids eat from little glass jars. The first foods they are fed have expiration dates far off in the future. Their food is devoid of anything that makes food satisfying and good. Their food is mass-produced and has no love. It is not the right path for our children.

The techniques and recipes in this book are not only easy, they are full of love.

Remember, it only takes one hour every two weeks.

3.
you can do it!

good ingredients

Good ingredients are essential to any recipe. In the restaurants we strive to buy the best products we can buy from great sources locally and all over the world. As you shop you should also look for the best products you can get. Here are some things to look for.

THE GROCERY STORE

Shop in places that you respect and enjoy being in. I love great grocery stores where the ingredients are vast and beautiful. Our kids love to go because there are so many things to see and smell and taste. If the store is run-down or the employees unhelpful, find someplace new. Why spend money in a place you don't enjoy being in? Look for a produce department that is well organized and clean. A butcher section that is spotless and well staffed and a fish section where you actually can see whole fish. Other great sources for great food include local farm stands, farmer's markets, your own garden, small butcher shops, and fish markets. Norah and I get our ingredients from our little garden, a fun Whole Foods down the road, a brand-new and fairly well-organized Safeway in town, a seasonal farmer's market that brings local farmers into the big city each Sunday, and even the behemoth Costco just outside of town. All have pros and cons but across the board all offer high-quality products.

THE OBVIOUS

While I don't completely understand why some people tap on melons, it isn't rocket science to pick stuff that looks and smells good. Green and leafy vegetables should never appear dry, wilted, or brown. Fruits should be aromatic and attractive. Ask to smell the fish before they wrap it up. It should smell like the bright blue ocean, not a stinky sewer. Red meats should appear red and fresh. Fresh chicken shouldn't be sitting in a pool of its own blood and should never appear partially frozen. Check the "sell by" date on anything that has it! Stores normally put the freshest stuff in the back, so reach back there and grab the best.

SEASONAL

I'm an advocate without being a fanatic of eating seasonally. Strawberries and asparagus in the spring. Corn and tomatoes and peaches in the summer. Squashes, apples, and pears in the fall. Root vegetables in the winter. The farms in the mid-Atlantic follow this classic seasonal calendar. Local seasonal produce tends to be cheaper due to high supply and lower transportation costs. It is a heck of a lot cheaper to bring an apple to Washington, D.C., from a field in Maryland than it is from a field in Chile. And for the most part, the faster you can get the food from the field to your kitchen . . . the better it tastes.

That all being said, I am not a fanatic on seasonality. South America provides North America with an opposite growing season. The asparagus coming from Chile during our fall is, well . . . pretty good. Similarly, it would almost be unthinkable for me to go the entire spring and summer without an apple. It is a handy and durable little fruit and holds up pretty well in shipping and storage. California and Florida and hydroponic agriculture offers us 365-day growing seasons on many items. And for the most part I think that is a good thing. At the same time, I pass on some seasonal items except when they can be found at their peak. A fresh peach in February just feels wrong and blueberries in November don't make sense to me or my palate.

LOCAL

Like my thoughts on seasonal . . . I'm an advocate of local without being fanatical. Get it if you can! If you live by the sea . . . by all means use the local fish. If you live in California you live nearest to a bounty of fruits and vegetables that are enjoyed all over the country and world. We love our local farmer's market and take advantage of it weekly for about half of the year. But local is often limited and I'm not going to forgo a banana just because I don't live in the tropics. There are valid arguments that involve everything from free trade, nutrition, economics, sustainability, and environmental impact. They are all valid discussions . . . and up to you to decide. Once again, I am an advocate, not a fanatic.

ORGANIC OR CONVENTIONAL?

This is certainly a topic that gets some people all riled up! Organic products are my first preference, especially for children's food. What is not to like? There are fewer hormones, few chemicals, and fewer pesticides. It is better for the earth and it all seems like a good thing.

In my mind the only downside is price. Organic food is almost always more expensive than its conventional counterparts. In fact, organic options are often too expensive for me to use in my restaurants. Hopefully, the price gap between organic and conventional will narrow as organic farming becomes bigger and better. But for now expect to pay more.

Some of the ingredients in this book are unavailable in organic form. Whole Foods certainly led the way in terms of selection, variety, and quality. Norah and I used organic foods when available and when they were comparable or better than nonorganic products. Our kids definitely got a mix.

In fact, my parents had never even heard of "organic" until I was a college graduate. Fruit was just fruit. So I don't subscribe to the notion that a conventional apple is exactly a poisonous one. That being said, there are some pretty compelling arguments to keep your baby's food as organic as possible.

Even though organic is often more expensive, the good news is that the overall amount you will need for your child is fairly small. And as you saw on page 11, whether you choose organic or conventional, you'll be saving a lot of dough compared to buying the mass-produced stuff in jars.

COMPARISON OF SOME PRICES AT MY LOCAL SUPERMARKET

Bananas	Organic $.98/lb	Conventional $.53/lb
Apples (Fuji)	Organic $.83/each	Conventional $.1.25/lb
Carrots (peeled "baby")	Organic $2.39/lb	Conventional $1.99/lb
Carrots (whole, unpeeled)	Organic $1.19/lb	Conventional $.99/lb
Yogurt	Organic $2.99/qt	Conventional $1.99/qt
Milk	Organic $5.79/gallon	Conventional $2.99/gallon
Whole chicken	Organic $3.29/lb	Conventional $1.99/lb

The strongest argument for buying organic for your child is that you know what is NOT in organic. Organic farming methods heavily reduce or eliminate the likelihood that unnatural chemicals and pesticides will be in the food your child will eat. I feel better leaving the skin on an apple when it is organic. Preparing baby food yourself is a great step towards the health of your child. Doing it with organic ingredients is clearly even better.

Sometimes the labeling can be a bit confusing. The USDA oversees organic food and labeling. According to the USDA, products labeled as "100 percent organic" must contain 100 percent organic ingredients. Products labeled "organic" must contain 95 percent organic ingredients. In both cases the product or package can include the USDA Organic logo.

If a product is labeled "made with organic ingredients," it must have at least 75 percent organic ingre-

dients but is not allowed to have the USDA Organic logo on the package. Labels that say "all natural," "free range," "no hormones added," etc., are not regulated by the USDA and it is often difficult to assess what it really means. They do not, however, imply that the product is organic. On the other hand organic doesn't imply that a food is particularly healthy. Organic butter has as many calories and as much fat as nonorganic butter. It is also important to note that while organic food is no more or less nutritious than conventional food, its primary benefit lies in the reduced amount of chemicals, pesticides, insecticides, antibiotics, and/or hormones. All of which is good for your kids.

Long story short . . . buy organic when you can.

FRESH OR FROZEN?

The answer for me is fresh with a small asterisk. I will always pick the fresh version if I can. But there are times when I will consider a frozen option. There are even a few cases when I actually prefer the frozen variety simply for the sake of speed and efficiency.

The primary advantage of some frozen produce is that they were picked ripe and then frozen. At times this can offer better quality and consistency than fresh. The secondary advantage is that someone else did the cleaning, peeling, and cutting. The downside is that they have been sitting in a bag in your grocer's freezer for who knows how long!

My favorite frozen fruits and vegetables to use in *Baby Love* purees are peas, mangoes, and peaches.

Fresh peas and peaches are tough to find perfectly ripe and both are a pain to prep. Fresh mangoes are tough to cut for novices and can vary in ripeness. Frozen blueberries and strawberries are okay. Always read the label. Make sure the package of peas says PEAS not PEAS, SALT. If it's peaches the ingredients should be PEACHES. I stay away from everything else in the frozen section.

CANNED?

Except for canned San Marzano tomatoes, canned vegetables and fruits are quite simply gross.

sanitation

Safe food handling is an essential part of creating food for anyone, especially your baby. Fortunately, safe food handling and sanitation practices are often simply a matter of common sense. Here are some chef tips to keep in mind when preparing food for your baby.

WASH YOUR HANDS!

The birth of a child reminds everyone of the importance of frequent hand washing. It is equally important when cooking. Twenty seconds with lots of soap and warm water. Dry with a clean and disposable paper towel (that damp dish towel is pretty sketchy to me). Wash them once before you get started. Wash them immediately after handling any raw poultry, meat, or fish. Wash them if you happen to touch your mouth, nose, eyes, etc. Wash them after touching any dirty or sandy vegetables or fruit. Wash them when you complete your cooking.

IF YOU ARE FEELING SICK!

Don't cook. Even though your l'il one will give you a dozen colds over the next few years, this is not the time for payback. Take the day off and come back to it when you are feeling well.

CROSS CONTAMINATION!

Your hands are the number-one source of cross contamination. Cross contamination occurs when you touch raw products like poultry, fish, and meat and then touch another ingredient. The same can happen with tongs, spoons, knives, and cutting boards. Make sure to wash anything that touches raw poultry, fish, and meat completely with hot water and soap before using it to touch another ingredient.

NO DOUBLE DIPPING!

It is like the *Seinfeld* episode! If you are spoon-feeding your baby from a small bowl and they don't finish the food . . . don't save it. The bacteria in the child's mouth gets on the spoon and then in the bowl. That bacteria can grow while the food is in the fridge and the next day it could be a veritable petri dish. The same goes when tasting the food while cooking. Always use a clean spoon for every taste.

COOLING BABY FOOD

Most of the baby food recipes in this book are designed to be poured into ice cube trays, wrapped, and frozen. If you do refrigerate any of the recipes make sure they are cooled to refrigerator temperature (about 40°F) within six hours. Eat any refrigerated purees within three days.

REHEATING FOOD FOR YOUR BABY

If you are reheating any of the recipes that contain meat, fish, or poultry, make sure it is heated to at least 165°F. Then let cool before serving.

HOW LONG CAN I STORE BABY FOOD?

Three days in the refrigerator. Three months in the freezer.

mise en place—everything in its place

Much of cooking is preparation. The motto at the Culinary Institute of America is "Preparation Is Everything." I was a boy scout as a kid, which meant "Be Prepared!" It is all good advice and essential for a good cook.

Mise en place is a phrase used often in professional kitchens. It is French for "Everything in its place." When you see a chef on television with bowls full of nicely prepared ingredients, that is his or her *mise en place*. The success of every cook in a professional kitchen is contingent on *mise en place*. Without it, the night is doomed. With it, the meal is destined for success. It is much the same for someone cooking at home.

Step One: *Mise en place* starts with a happy and ready work environment. I like to turn on all the lights and put on some good tunes. Next, I make sure the area is clean and organized. I clean the sink and countertop. I empty the dishwasher and take out the garbage.

Step Two: The next step for achieving perfect *mise en place* is to set up your equipment. On pages 27 to 30 I provide a comprehensive list of equipment you will need to make almost every recipe in this book. Remember to get everything out before proceeding. Ducking in and out of cabinets and drawers during the cooking process slows the process down. Speed is your friend when cooking.

Get in the habit of always putting commonly used items in the same place. For example, a cutting board should always have a specific spot on the counter. Think about your space and what should go

where. If you use an item, say a peeler, put it back in the same location after using it. This takes discipline but will make you a better cook. This is also the step in which you should preheat ovens if necessary.

Finally you'll need to set up a bag or pail for garbage. I use a paper grocery bag next to the counter where I do my cutting.

Step Three: The penultimate step to get your *mise en place* together is getting the food out. Pull out ALL the food you need for the recipe you are working on. Remove plastic bags, rubber bands, ties, etc. Once again, don't underestimate the hassle of going in and out of refrigerators and your pantry when cooking a recipe. It will take you away from your primary focus—executing the recipe as fast and as accurately as possible.

Step Four: The final step is the washing, cutting, and measuring. These steps will be found in each recipe. Once completed you will have your *mise en place*. The cooking will be easy.

Proper mise en place enabled me to cook the twins' food in about one hour every two weeks.

equipment

You don't need to have a professionally equipped kitchen to make baby food. However, it does help to have some solid, sturdy tools. When buying anything for my kitchen I look for stuff that will last. Sometimes it costs a bit more, but in the long run it is worth it. I also stay away from anything too "gadgety." I remember an apple slicer in my house growing up. It cored and sliced an apple into wedges simultaneously. A good knife can usually do the task of most kitchen gadgets!

My favorite sources for equipment: Sur La Table and Williams Sonoma are excellent stores. Target and Costco have good stuff cheap. Everything is available on Amazon and you don't have to leave your house. Our family must be Amazon's best customer. For people who want commercial cooking equipment at home, I recommend going to www.webstaurantstore.com.

BLENDER

If it makes margaritas it will make any puree in this book. And as a new parent I highly recommend making a frozen margarita once in a while! The recipe for that is on page 132. Seriously. In my house and in the restaurants I use a Vita-Prep. It is a monster of a machine. Truly a blender on steroids. It is way too expensive for most home-kitchen use. Just try to use something with about a 48-ounce or more jar capacity. Otherwise you may have to puree some of the bigger recipes in two batches.

KNIFE #1

I recommend using an 8- or 9-inch chef's knife. I use a Wusthof Grand Prix and have been using it for more than ten years. There are many good knives out there—the serrated Ginsu knife for $19.95 is not one of them! I don't care if it can cut through a can and then a tomato! A good chef's knife has to have an edge that can be sharpened, and serrated chef's knives cannot be sharpened. A good chef's knife can be bought for between $30 and $100. My Wusthof cost about $75. It may seem expensive but a good chef's knife will last twenty years or more if well treated.

KNIFE #2

Get a nice 4-inch paring knife with an edge that can be sharpened. You can find something decent for $5 to $15. I keep three or four non-name brand ones around the kitchen.

SHARPENER AND STEEL

Most people have never sharpened their knives in their lives. Problem is that a dull knife is the most dangerous. A dull knife tends to slide away from what you are supposed to be cutting and ends up making a nice little mark in your finger. To see how to sharpen and steel a knife correctly just go to www.babylovepurees.com and click on "Sharpening a Knife" under "Videos."

CUTTING BOARDS

I find it helpful to have a few cutting boards in the kitchen. I use a 24 × 18-inch Boos and Company wood board and two 18 × 12-inch plastic cutting boards. The plastic ones are really easy to clean.

MELON BALLER

One of the few "gadgety" devices I allow in my kitchen. This tool is great for getting cores out of apples

and pears without any waste. A decent one will run about $10.

POTS

Most of the baby recipes in this book use a 4-quart pot. I use a 4-quart All-Clad sauce pan with a lid. It is expensive (about $175) but will last a lifetime . . . or two. A slightly smaller and/or less heavy-duty pot would work, too. Most of these recipes aren't really demanding.

WOODEN SPOONS

I am a fan of the 13-inch Beechwood spoons imported from France. They are a culinary classic and cost about $5.

RUBBER SPATULAS

Essential for scraping down the sides of pots to get everything from the pots to the blender and from the blender to the storage container. Spatulas eliminate waste. Any sturdy rubber or silicone spatula will do. Typical cost about $5.

MEASURING CUP

I like a good clear plastic 1-pint measuring cup. I use a Rubbermaid product that costs about $8.

MEASURING SPOONS

Just something simple. I only use the tablespoon and teaspoon. Everything else is pretty frivolous. Remember 1 tablespoon equals 3 teaspoons.

KITCHEN TOWELS

I keep one near the range to pick up hot pots. I keep another next to my cutting board to clean off knives, tools, and cutting boards. And I use one more, wet, to wipe down any spills and drips.

LARGE MIXING BOWLS

A few large mixing bowls will come in handy when setting up ice baths for blanching and shocking green vegetables. They can be glass, plastic, or stainless steel. I prefer stainless.

COLANDER OR STRAINER

A decent medium-sized strainer or colander is sufficient.

ICE CUBE TRAYS

Get lots of ice cube trays! There are all sorts of cutie patootie trays for baby food. I prefer the white Rubbermaid ones with sixteen little cubes. They are cheap and easy and hold about 32 ounces of purees per tray, making each cube 2 ounces.

STORAGE CONTAINER

Make sure you have about a dozen 48-ounce (or so) storage containers with a good lid. The disposable/reusable ones are pretty effective. These are good to store recipes that you don't need to freeze.

SHEET TRAYS

Home cooks call these cookie sheets. I keep two of these around and use the 18 × 13-inch size. If you want the commercial quality ones at a cheap price you can get them online. My favorite restaurant supply store is www.webstaurantstore.com.

TONGS

Nine- or 12-inch utility tongs are essential to all good cooks. They are a heat-resistant extension of your hand.

LARGE METAL SPOON

Great for scraping out butternut squash seeds or getting the sweet potato out of the skin.

PEELER

A good peeler is easy to find. About $4.

PARCHMENT PAPER

Will save you clean up time!

PLASTIC WRAP AND GALLON ZIPLOC BAGS

Buy in bulk.

MASKING TAPE AND BLACK SHARPIE

For labeling and dating.

the fundamentals

The chef-instructors at the Culinary Institute of America frequently remind students that they are not there to learn to be "creative" but rather to learn "fundamentals." "Only with the mastery of fundamental skills," they would argue, "can one truly be creative." Fortunately the fundamental techniques for creating *Baby Love* recipes are easy. With just a little knowledge you'll be venturing beyond the recipes included here and creating your own.

Ninety-five percent of cooking is done using eight fairly simple techniques.

poaching · braising · roasting · frying · steaming
boiling · sautéing · grilling

The first six are the focus in this book. We'll leave out frying for the sake of Junior's cholesterol level. Imagine . . . Baby's First Bloomin' Onion . . . not exactly pediatrician approved. I'll also leave out grilling. While it is certainly a healthy cooking method there is something incongruous about Mesquite Grilled Butternut Squash Puree.

There are variations of the eight major techniques like broiling (upside-down grilling), stewing (braising, but small pieces), baking (a blander-sounding synonym for roasting), stir-frying (essentially sauté), simmering (slow and gentle boil), and a few others. Mastering these fundamental techniques makes us good cooks and allows food to be prepared in infinitely inventive ways.

Here are some quick definitions of the major techniques we will be using in *Baby Love*, plus a quick review of how to puree properly and safely . . .

POACHING

A moist heat cooking method in which tender ingredients are cooked in warm (about 160°F), often flavorful liquid, and allowed to cook very gently for a relatively short period of time. This works best with tender fish and chicken. You'll see this method used in the Halibut and Peas and Salmon and Carrot recipes.

STEAMING

A moist heat cooking method in which ingredients are cooked with a small amount of liquid heated until the liquid is converted to steam. The steam must be trapped—usually by a lid. You'll see this method throughout the book.

BRAISING

A moist heat cooking method in which typically tough cuts of meat are slowly cooked for long periods while partially submerged in a flavorful liquid. You'll see this method in the Slow Beef Stew.

BOILING

A moist heat cooking method in which ingredients are put into very hot (212°F) liquid. You'll see this technique used regularly throughout the book when preparing green vegetables in the blanching process. Simmering is the more gentle variation of boiling and occurs at temperatures approaching 200°F (more than a poach, less than a boil).

ROASTING

A dry heat cooking method in which ingredients are cooked with indirect heat. You'll see this healthy technique used in favorites like sweet potato and butternut squash where caramelization of the ingredients gives a more complex flavor to the final product than if you had simply boiled them in water.

SAUTÉING

A dry heat cooking method in which ingredients are cooked very quickly in a pan in a little bit of butter, oil, or fat. It is definitely the most popular method of cooking in my restaurants. It is less popular in this book but I encourage parents to understand this method well. As the baby transitions into finger foods it is a great way to whip up diced or julienned meats and vegetables.

PUREEING

There is A LOT of pureeing in this book so it is important to review a few tips on using a blender properly and safely.

1. If the ingredients are really hot you must start the blender on the lowest level. Slowly work your way up to a more aggressive speed. That will prevent you from decorating your kitchen ceiling with sweet potatoes. And always use the lid.

2. If the ingredients are not blending, turn off the machine and use a wooden spoon to reposition the ingredients. Try to get the liquids near the blades. Replace the cover and turn the machine back on. DO NOT put a spoon or a spatula into the machine while it is running. And of course NEVER stick your hand in there when the machine is plugged in. It sounds obvious but I am just reminding you.

3. If the puree seems too thick, add a little water or liquid. If a puree seems too thin, you can usually add a bit of oatmeal or rice cereal to thicken it up. These can also be added each time you heat up the ice cubes of the puree for your child.

storing *baby love* purees

The majority of the recipes in this book are designed to be frozen and stored until it is time for your baby to eat. The process is simple. Just pour the purees from the blender into the ice cube tray and allow to cool. Wrap in plastic wrap and freeze overnight. The next day unwrap and pop the purees out. Store in a Ziploc bag. Label and date with masking tape. (Once you start filling up the freezer with *Baby Love* purees you'll be thankful that you labeled everything. Is that carrot or sweet potato? Maybe it's butternut?) When it is time to eat, pull out a few cubes and heat them up in the microwave or on the stove top.

I highly recommend storing *Baby Love* purees in the freezer. It prevents waste and guarantees freshness. Of course if you still have a dozen flavors of Häagen-Dazs ice cream left over from the pregnancy you might run out of space quickly. If you are storing purees or other recipes for your baby in the refrigerator, I recommend a "three and out policy." Use it within three days or get rid of it. In the restaurant we say . . . "When in doubt, throw it out." If you keep sniffing it and smelling it and asking your spouse, "Hey, honey, do you think this is still all right?" it isn't.

4.

let's cook

fruits

perfectly basic apple

continued

- YIELD 34 OUNCES
- 6 MONTHS PLUS

INGREDIENTS
5 apples
8 ounces water or apple
   juice

Wash and peel fruit (peeling is optional).

Cut each apple in half.

Remove the seeds and stem with a melon baller.

Cut each half into 6 pieces.

Put the apple pieces and the water or apple juice into a 4-quart pot.

Turn the burner on high and cover with a lid.

Cook for approximately 8 minutes, stirring once. The apples should be tender but not mushy.

Pour everything into the blender. Puree until smooth.

Pour into two ice cube trays and allow to cool.

Wrap and freeze until ready to serve.

chef's notes

Waste Not Want Not . . . I use a melon baller to remove the seeds and stems because it maximizes the yield of the apple. A good chef is naturally a cheap chef—let's say frugal.

nutrition tip

The old saying "An apple a day keeps the doctor away" is certainly true. Apples are vitamin-packed. They are also an excellent source of fiber and studies show their flavonoids help prevent heart disease and many cancers.

To Peel or Not to Peel?

Here's my take. If the apple is organic or fresh from an orchard and doesn't have all sorts of waxy buildup on the outside, I say leave the skin on. It is easier and the peel is full of nutrients and fiber and stuff. If you are unsure, peel it. One benefit from peeling is that you get this gorgeous creamy white puree when making apple or pear purees. Of course if you leave the skin on you get cool colors depending on the type of apple. Leaving the skin on also gives you a better yield.

Fiji, Gala, Granny, Braeburn, Mac, Oh My!

There are lots of apples in the grocery store. Don't panic. They all taste pretty good. Buy what looks fresh. Buy what is in season. Heck, buy what is cheap! It really doesn't matter. I have used just about every type of apple. The only one that resulted in some push back from the l'il ones was with Granny Smiths. They are pretty tart. If you have them . . . mix 'em with some other ones to balance out the sweet and the tart.

pom-pom apple

• 6 MONTHS PLUS

Follow instructions for Perfectly Basic Apple but use 100 percent pomegranate juice instead of the water or apple juice.

nutrition tip

Pomegranates are some of the most nutritious fruits you can eat. Pomegranate juice is high in three different types of polyphenols, a potent form of antioxidants. These three types—tannins, anthocyanins, and ellagic acid—are credited with helping in the prevention of cancer and heart disease.

perfectly basic pear

- YIELD 36 OUNCES
- 6 MONTHS PLUS

INGREDIENTS

5 pears
6 ounces water or apple
  juice

Wash and peel fruit (peeling is optional).

Cut each pear in half.

Remove the seeds and stem with a melon baller.

Cut each half into 6 pieces.

Put the pear and the water or apple juice into a 4-quart pot.

Turn the burner on high and cover with a lid.

Cook for approximately 8 minutes, stirring once.

Pour everything into the blender. Puree until smooth.

Pour into two ice cube trays and allow to cool.

Wrap and freeze.

chef's notes

Bosc, D'Anjou, Bartlett! There are lots of pears in the grocery store. Bosc are tall and elegant with light brown skin. D'Anjou are fat and sweet with red or green skin. Bartlett have a classic pear shape with yellow to green skin. They are all good.

I'm 10 Months Mama-I Don't Eat Baby Food Anymore! All *Baby Love* Perfectly Basic recipes are the real go-to through the entire six to twelve months. There are ten total: Apple, Pear, Banana, Peach, Mango, Carrot, Sweet Potato, Pea, Butternut, and Avocado. They are aptly named "Perfectly Basic" because they are both perfect and basic. They are simple and really quick to make. Just because baby is ten months doesn't mean you should stop making the basics—sometimes they are the favorites and make meal time easier. My fourteen-month-old, Riley, is still

continued

willing to eat these simple recipes alongside whole green beans, carrot sticks, pizza, yogurt, roasted turkey, and whole strawberries! It is still great nutrition. As they get older you can puree less and less.

Cutting Consistency for Cooking This is not rocket science but just as a reminder . . . cut your fruit into approximately even pieces before cooking. That will ensure consistent cooking.

pom-pom pear

• 6 MONTHS PLUS

Follow instructions for Perfectly Basic Pear, but use 100 percent pomegranate juice instead of the water or apple juice.

nutrition tip
Pears are excellent sources of dietary fiber and Vitamin C. Fiber reduces constipation.

perfectly basic peach, 1

- YIELD 34 OUNCES
- 6 MONTHS PLUS

INGREDIENTS

2 pounds frozen peaches
   (that's usually two bags)
6 ounces water

Put the peaches and water in a 4-quart pot.

Turn the burner on high and cover with a lid.

Cook for approximately 6 to 7 minutes, stirring once.

Pour everything into the blender. Puree until smooth.

Pour into two ice cube trays and allow to cool.

Wrap and freeze.

chef's notes

Fresh versus Frozen This recipe is super fast. You don't even need a knife! I recommend using frozen peaches because they are peeled, ripe, and really really easy. Did I remember to say it was easy? You are a new parent—give yourself a break once in a while. Use frozen peaches that have no other ingredients other than PEACHES in the package. Do not use canned peaches. I hate cans . . . unless they are full of beer or San Marzano tomatoes. I'm also a fan of frozen peas, mangoes, and blueberries. Okay, okay, you and your baby are from the great state of Georgia . . . turn the page and I'll give you a PERFECTLY BASIC PEACH recipe for fresh summer peaches.

nutrition tip
Peaches are packed with potassium, antioxidants, Vitamin A, Vitamin C, and beta-carotene.

perfectly basic peach, 2

- YIELD 34 OUNCES
- 6 MONTHS PLUS

INGREDIENTS

5 fresh and ripe peaches
  (about 2½ pounds total)

6 ounces water

Wash and peel fruit (peeling is optional).

Cut each peach in half by running a paring knife from the stem to the base and back up to the stem again. Grab each side and twist in opposite directions. One side should come out clean and the other should have a pit in it. If the peach is ripe, the pit should come right out. If the peach is unripe the pit will need to be cut out carefully with a paring knife.

Turn each half onto the cutting board round side up.

Cut each half into 4 pieces.

Put the peaches and water in a 4-quart pot.

Turn the burner on high and cover with a lid.

Cook for approximately 6 to 7 minutes, stirring once.

Pour everything into the blender. Puree until smooth.

Pour into two ice cube trays and allow to cool.

Wrap and freeze

chef's notes

If Your Peaches Aren't Ripe Let them sit on the countertop for a few days. They will ripen up.

perfectly basic mango

"ANOTHER OF THE WORLD'S EASIEST RECIPES"

- YIELD 36 OUNCES
- 6 MONTHS PLUS

INGREDIENTS

2 pounds frozen mangoes
(that's usually two bags)

8 ounces water

Put the mangoes and water in a 4-quart pot.

Turn the burner on high and cover with a lid.

Cook for approximately 7 minutes, stirring once.

Pour everything into the blender. Puree until smooth. It will become "silky smooth."

Pour into two ice cube trays and allow to cool.

Wrap and freeze.

chef's notes

If you want to use fresh . . . pick ripe mangoes (slightly soft to the touch). You'll need approximately 4 mangoes to yield 2 pounds of usable fruit. Peel the mango with a peeler.

nutrition tip
Mangoes are rich in vitamins A and C, both important antioxidant nutrients.

perfectly basic banana

- YIELD 1 SERVING
- 6 MONTHS PLUS
- A 90-SECOND RECIPE

INGREDIENTS

½ banana,
   the riper the better

Place banana on a cutting board.

Mash with the back of a fork for 90 seconds.

The banana will be completely smooth.

This is a nonfreezing recipe.

nutrition tip
Bananas are super baby foods. They are rich in carbohydrates, vitamins, and potassium. They help with both constipation and loose stools.

banana apple pear

- YIELD 36 OUNCES
- 6 MONTHS PLUS

INGREDIENTS

1 pear

2 apples

3 bananas peeled and
each cut into 3 pieces

8 ounces apple juice or
water

2 tablespoons flaxseed,
ground

Wash and peel pear and apples
(peeling is optional).

Cut pear and apples in half.

Remove the seeds and stem with a melon baller.

Cut each half into 6 pieces.

Put the pear and the apple and the water into a 4-quart pot.

Turn the burner on high and cover with a lid.

Cook for approximately 7 minutes, stirring once.

Add the bananas and the flaxseed.

Stir well and cook an additional 1 minute. Stir during the remaining minute of cooking.

Pour everything into the blender. Puree until smooth.

Pour into two ice cube trays and allow to cool.

Wrap and freeze.

chef's notes

Our amazing nanny, Alba, gently reminds the kids "No Messy" as she helps them keep their faces and hands clean while eating. A good chef is always cleaning. When the fruit is cooking take the time to tidy up around you and prepare for the next recipe. Just after pouring the cooked contents from the pot to the blender, take a quick moment to pour some cold water in the pot, especially in a recipe with a starch like oatmeal, flaxseed, or wheat germ. Trust me, it will make cleanup easier if you are always thinking "No Messy."

Norah has been quoted in the press as being able to cook two things: BLTs and banana bread. While she has never played the role of the primary cook in our family, her repertoire has grown a bit over the years. That being said, Norah remains a banana bread aficionado and she enjoys eating this recipe as much as the kids, because it tastes so much like banana bread! Her BLTs are really good, too. She is a real believer in extra mayo and extra bacon. She makes a chef proud.

chef's notes

Henry's first favorite food was bananas. It is the perfect food—loaded with energy. I have watched my kids eat two or three bananas in a row. They are little monkeys! If you ever have bananas that are becoming a little too ripe, simply peel them and stick 'em in the freezer. They work great for recipes like this one.

Water or Juice? Here's my take. I like the apple juice. It puts a few more calories into the dish. Calories keep the baby satiated and thus Mommy and Daddy get some sleep. Only use 100 percent juice with no added anything—especially sugar. On the other hand, a lot of doctors and baby dentists are cautious about juice when the baby gets a bit older. As I said before, I usually took the juice route and got me some ZZZs.

papaya banana

"TROPICAL DELIGHT THAT'S GOOD FOR THE TUMMY"

- YIELD 38–44 OUNCES
- 6 MONTHS PLUS

INGREDIENTS

2 meridol papayas
  (about 4 to 4½ pounds
  total)

8 ounces water

3 bananas peeled and
  each cut into 3 pieces

Slice each papaya in half lengthwise.

Remove the dark seeds with a spoon.

Cut each half into quarters lengthwise (you'll have 16 pieces total).

Lay each piece on a cutting board with fruit side up and peel down.

Carefully, carve off the good pink fruit from the skin like you would a watermelon. Dice each strip into 4 pieces.

Put the papaya and water in a 4-quart pot.

Turn the burner on high and cover with a lid.

Cook for approximately 4 minutes, stirring once.

Add the bananas and stir while cooking for an additional 1 minute.

Pour everything into the blender. Puree until smooth. It will become "silky smooth."

Pour into two ice cube trays and allow to cool.

Wrap and freeze.

chef's notes

Meridol papayas are pretty big. They are about 2 to 2.5 pounds apiece. Meridol papayas are not particularly sweet but they are known for helping digestion. I pair them up with ripe bananas to enhance the sweetness and make them more desirable to the little ones.

perfectly basic avocado "BABY AVOCADO"

- YIELD 1 SERVING
- A 90-SECOND RECIPE
- 6 MONTHS PLUS

INGREDIENTS

½ avocado, nice and ripe
  but not all brown

1 tablespoon orange juice

Mash the avocado with the back of a fork for 90 seconds.

The avocado will be completely smooth and creamy. Mix in the orange juice to sweeten.

This is a nonfreezing recipe.

chef's notes

To cut an avocado in half insert the blade of a chef's knife into the avocado lengthwise until you hit the pit. Keeping the knife still, rotate the avocado until you have made a cut to the pit from top to bottom and back again. Twist the two halves in opposite directions to separate. One side will have a pit. Using the bottom of the blade (closest to the handle) hit the center of the pit once and then twist the pit out and discard. Scoop the flesh out with a spoon.

Convert the second half of the avocado into a quick guacamole snack. Just add 4 to 6 leaves of chopped cilantro, a tiny bit of chopped onion, a squeeze from ¼ lime, and some salt and pepper. Eat with chips or use as a spread on a sandwich.

nutrition tip

Avocados are a nutrient-dense fruit. Their high-carbohydrate and protein content make them an ideal food for babies. They also have nearly twenty vitamins, minerals, and phytonutrients. Phytonutrients are thought to help prevent many chronic diseases.

apple prune "APPLE A LA TOULOUSE LAUTREC"

- YIELD 32 OUNCES
- 8 MONTHS PLUS

INGREDIENTS
4 apples
10 prunes (dried plums)
10 ounces water or apple juice

Wash and peel the apples (peeling is optional).

Cut each apple in half.

Remove the seeds and stem with a melon baller.

Cut each half into 6 pieces.

Check each prune for pits.

Put the apple pieces, prunes, and juice into a 4-quart pot.

Turn the burner on high and cover with a lid.

Cook for approximately 8 minutes, stirring once.

Pour everything into the blender. Puree until smooth.

Pour into two ice cube trays and allow to cool.

Wrap and freeze.

chef's notes

When I was a kid we had a golden retriever named Lautrec. The dog was named after the French painter Toulouse Lautrec. He got the name because as a puppy he pooped too much—he was literally "Too Loose." Poop becomes a powerful force in a home with a baby. It is a topic of conversation. Parents study it. Equipment is purchased to contain it and diapers are an hourly chore. And honestly it doesn't get much better with toddlers. This recipe will keep baby "regular."

Prunes are the number-one source of antioxidants and also are good for the prevention and relief of constipation.

cinnamon apple oatmeal raisin "IT TASTES LIKE APPLE PIE"

- YIELD 36 OUNCES
- 8 MONTHS PLUS

INGREDIENTS

4 apples

½ cup golden raisins

¼ teaspoon ground cinnamon

12 ounces water or apple juice

½ cup baby oatmeal cereal

Wash and peel the apples (peeling is optional).

Cut each apple in half.

Remove the seeds and stem with a melon baller.

Cut each half into 6 pieces.

Put the apple pieces, raisins, cinnamon, and water into a 4-quart pot.

Turn the burner on high and cover with a lid.

Cook for approximately 7 minutes, stirring once.

Add the oatmeal and cook for 1 more minute, stirring throughout the final minute.

Pour everything into the blender. Puree until smooth.

Pour into two ice cube trays and allow to cool.

Wrap and freeze.

chef's notes

Baby Gets a Little Spice! Aromatics make food delightful. Just because your little one is eight months old doesn't mean life needs to be bland.

Watch the Dried Fruits or Be Prepared to Scrub . . . I use dried fruits in a number of recipes. When I do, I increase the amount of liquid in the recipe. This prevents the recipe from burning the bottom of your pot. Keep an extra eye on recipes that have dried fruit to make sure they don't cook down too quickly. It is a mess to clean if they do.

But I Only Have Regular Raisins! It is just a recipe . . . modify it any way you want. That's cooking!

very blueberry and apple

"AKA . . DON'T EAT THIS ON THE WHITE CARPET BLUEBERRY APPLE"

- YIELD 32 OUNCES
- 8 MONTHS PLUS

INGREDIENTS

4 apples

1 cup fresh blueberries

8 ounces water or
  apple juice

Wash and peel the apples (peeling is optional).

Cut each apple in half.

Remove the seeds and stem with a melon baller.

Cut each half into 6 pieces.

Look over blueberries for stems.

Put the apple pieces, blueberries, and juice into a 4-quart pot.

Turn the burner on high and cover with a lid.

Cook for approximately 8 minutes, stirring once.

Pour everything into the blender. Puree until smooth.

Pour into two ice cube trays and allow to cool.

Wrap and freeze.

chef's notes

Knowing the antioxidant power of blueberries I tried to make a blueberry puree. Whoa. It was so strong. Henry, acting as the tester, gave it a big rejection by gagging. Blueberries are powerful and need something to balance them. Pears and peaches would work well.

nutrition tip
Blueberries are packed with big health benefits like lots of antioxidants that can prevent cancers.

apricot pear "A IS FOR APRICOT"

- YIELD 36 OUNCES
- 8 MONTHS PLUS

INGREDIENTS

4 pears

1 cup dried apricots
(about 20 pieces)

6 ounces apple juice
or water

Wash and peel the pears (peeling is optional).

Cut each pear in half.

Remove the seeds and stem with a melon baller.

Cut each half into 6 pieces.

Check the apricots for pits.

Put the pears, apricots, and juice into a 4-quart pot.

Turn the burner on high and cover with a lid.

Cook for approximately 8 minutes, stirring once.

Pour everything into the blender. Puree until smooth.

Pour into two ice cube trays and allow to cool.

Wrap and freeze.

chef's notes

Sulfur Allergy A lot of the very pretty and bright orange dried apricots you see in the stores have been treated with sulfur in the drying process. My kids have eaten apricots both with and without the sulfur. I think I'd err on the side of caution here and start them off with the unsulfured kind.

nutrition tip
Apricots are rich in beta-carotene and are also a good source of iron and potassium. As Chef Geoff says, just make sure your dried apricots are not treated with sulfur dioxide. It can cause a reaction in babies.

peach and apricot oatmeal

• YIELD 32 OUNCES

• 8 MONTHS PLUS

INGREDIENTS

2 pounds frozen peaches
(that's usually two bags)

1 cup dried apricots
(about 20 apricots)

20 ounces water

½ cup baby oatmeal
cereal

Put the peaches, apricots, and water in a 4-quart pot.

Turn the burner on high and cover with a lid.

Cook for approximately 7 minutes, stirring once.

Add the oatmeal cereal and stir while cooking for an additional 1 minute.

Pour everything into the blender. Puree until smooth.

Pour into two ice cube trays and allow to cool.

Wrap and freeze.

chef's notes

We bought special baby oatmeal cereal for all three kids. It was what we fed them after they proved themselves to be good with the rice cereal. In my opinion it is one of those items that the baby food companies make to take advantage of frazzled new parents. After a while I just took some quick-cooking rolled oats and chopped them into dust in a food processor.

baby guacamole

- YIELD 4 SERVINGS
- 8 MONTHS PLUS
- A 120-SECOND RECIPE

INGREDIENTS

1 avocado, nice and ripe but not all brown

⅓ lime

1 tablespoon cilantro, chopped well

1 tablespoon minced red or yellow onion

Remove the pit from the avocado and scoop out the flesh from the peel.

Place the avocado on a cutting board and squeeze the juice from the lime onto the avocado.

Sprinkle the avocado with cilantro and onion.

Mash with the back of a fork until completely smooth and creamy.

chef's notes

This is a restaurant-style guacamole recipe minus the salt. So feel free to make a larger batch, get a bag of chips, give baby a big bear hug, and watch some football together.

strawberry and fig

- YIELD 32 OUNCES
- 10 MONTHS PLUS

INGREDIENTS

8 ounces dried figs, cut
  in half, stems removed
  (about 12 figs)
1 pound strawberries,
  stems removed, washed
8 ounces water
⅓ cup baby oatmeal cereal

Put the figs, strawberries, and water in a 4-quart pot.

Turn the burner on high and cover with a lid.

Cook for approximately 5 minutes, stirring once.

Add the oatmeal cereal and stir while cooking for an additional 1 minute.

Pour everything into the blender. Puree until smooth.

Pour into two ice cube trays and allow to cool.

Wrap and freeze.

Figs are high in fiber and also a good source of potassium.

nutrition tip

Strawberries are full of Vitamin C and can help strengthen your baby's immunity. They also contain ellagic acid, which may prevent cancer. Watch for possible allergic reactions, as some babies are sensitive to berries like strawberries, blackberries, and raspberries.

strawberry banana pineapple

- YIELD 36 OUNCES
- 10 MONTHS PLUS

INGREDIENTS
1½ pounds strawberries
3 bananas
¼ pineapple
8 ounces water

Remove stems of strawberries and then wash the berries.

Cut each banana into 4 to 5 pieces.

Cut the pineapple—see demo below. Cut into pieces approximately the size of the strawberries.

Put everything into a 4-quart pot.

Turn the burner on high and cover with a lid.

Cook for approximately 6 minutes, stirring once.

Pour everything from the pot into a strainer with a bowl underneath to save the juice.

Pour the cooked fruit into the blender. Puree until smooth using 2 to 4 ounces of the reserved juice if necessary to adjust consistency.

Pour into two ice cube trays and allow to cool.

Wrap and freeze.

cran-orange

- YIELD 38 OUNCES
- 10 MONTHS PLUS

INGREDIENTS

4 pears

1 cup unsweetened cranberries, fresh or frozen

6 ounces orange juice

Wash the fruit and peel the pears (peeling is optional).

Cut each pear in half.

Remove the seeds and stem with a melon baller.

Cut each half into 6 pieces.

Put the pears, cranberries, and juice into a 4-quart pot.

Turn the burner on high and cover with a lid.

Cook for approximately 8 minutes, stirring once.

Pour everything into the blender. Puree until smooth.

Pour into two ice cube trays and allow to cool.

Wrap and freeze.

chef's notes

Cranberries are a very tart fruit and need the sweetness of the pear and orange juice you will find in this recipe.

You can add a little holiday spice to this one as well . . . add ¼ teaspoon of ground nutmeg.

You can also make this recipe with unsweetened dried cranberries in place of the fresh or frozen ones. Use ⅓ of a cup if using dried.

Try this with some freshly roasted turkey . . . it is really good!

nutrition tip

Cranberries are among the top foods with proven health benefits. They are full of antioxidants.

berry smoothie

- YIELD 16 OUNCES
- 10 MONTHS PLUS

INGREDIENTS

8 ounces yogurt, whole
  milk, plain

4 ounces frozen
  blueberries (that's ¼ of
  a 1-pound bag)
  4 ounces frozen
  strawberries (that's ¼ of
  a 1-pound bag)

½ frozen banana

1 teaspoon vanilla extract

2 ounces orange juice,
  as needed

Combine all ingredients in the blender and puree for 60 seconds.

Use the orange juice if the blender is having difficulty pureeing the ingredients.

Serve immediately.

feelin' peachy smoothie

- YIELD 16 OUNCES
- 10 MONTHS PLUS

INGREDIENTS

8 ounces yogurt, whole
milk, plain

8 ounces frozen peaches
(that's ½ of a 1-pound
bag)

4 dried apricots, cut into
quarters

½ frozen banana

1 teaspoon vanilla extract

2 ounces orange juice,
as needed

Combine all ingredients in the blender and puree for 60 seconds.

Use the orange juice if the blender is having difficulty pureeing the ingredients.

Serve immediately.

tropical smoothie

- YIELD 16 OUNCES
- 10 MONTHS PLUS

INGREDIENTS

8 ounces yogurt, whole milk, plain

4 ounces frozen mangoes (that's ¼ of a 1-pound bag)

4 ounces frozen pineapple (that's ¼ of a 1-pound bag)

½ frozen banana

1 teaspoon vanilla extract

2 ounces orange juice, as needed

Combine all ingredients in the blender and puree for 60 seconds.

Use the orange juice if the blender is having difficulty pureeing the ingredients.

Serve immediately.

chef's notes

I use up overripened bananas for smoothie recipes. Simply peel, put in a Ziploc bag, and freeze. Take them out as needed. It is important that all the fruit is frozen for the smoothie recipe. The colder it is served the better it tastes.

Smoothies all pretty much work the same way. The ratio is 8 ounces of yogurt, to 8 ounces of frozen fruit, and a half of a banana. The banana acts as the thickener. I use vanilla to give the smoothie a touch of extra flavor but it is not essential to the recipe. You can also use different juices. Feel free to experiment with your own fruits by keeping the ratio approximately eight to eight to half.

I designed this recipe for 16 ounces. That's about 4 ounces for your baby and about 12 ounces for you. It is a pretty good way to get your mojo going in the morning.

We use only whole-milk plain yogurt for the babies. It has no added sugar or artificial sweeteners. We buy it by the quart. It makes for a great snack as your child gets to about ten months and beyond.

veggies

perfectly basic pea

- YIELD 32 OUNCES
- 6 MONTHS PLUS

INGREDIENTS

1½ pounds frozen peas
 (that's usually 1½ bags)

8 ounces water

Fill a 4-quart pot halfway with water. Bring to a rolling boil over high heat.

While water is coming to a boil, get your "green veggie shocking station" ready. You'll need:

- Colander

- Large bowl filled with ice and cold water. You want as much ice as possible.

Pour the frozen peas into the colander. Run cool water over them to get rid of any ice crystals (which will allow the boiling water to come back to a boil faster).

Pour the peas into the boiling water. Cook for 3 minutes on highest heat.

Pour peas into colander. Run cold water over them and pour them into the ice bath. Allow the peas to chill for 3 minutes. Pour the peas back into the colander and pick out any remaining ice. (See photo, opposite page.)

Pour peas in the blender and add 8 ounces of cold water. Puree until smooth.

Pour into two ice cube trays.

Wrap and freeze.

chef's notes

Go GREEN! Peas (and all green veggies) should be bright green when cooked. The "green veggie shocking station" is critical to making your green veggies bright and beautiful instead of brown and drab. This technique works great for asparagus, green beans, broccoli, spinach, and really any green veggie. It's all about saving the chlorophyll in these vegetables. The chlorophyll is like little

continued

deflated balloons in the vegetable. When heated the balloons begin to expand. If the veggie is exposed to heat over too long a period the chlorophyll "balloons" will pop and all the green will spill out of the vegetable. Lots of nutrients are lost, too. When you bring the peas out of the boiling water and "shock them" in iced water you freeze the balloons just before they pop, and maximize the green!

Ambience In the restaurants, I am nuts about lighting and music. It is such an essential part of ambience. Create the right ambience when you are making *Baby Love* purees. Crank up all the lights in the kitchen. Put on some music that fits your mood. It will make your cooking so much more enjoyable!

nutrition tip

Green peas are a good source of Vitamin K, which is important for maintaining bone health. Peas also contain folic acid and Vitamin B$_6$, both good for heart health.

perfectly basic carrot

- YIELD 38 OUNCES
- 6 MONTHS PLUS

INGREDIENTS
1½ pounds carrots
20 ounces water
 (that's 2½ cups)

Pour the water into the pot and put on high heat.

Wash and then peel the carrots.

Cut off the stems and discard.

Cut the carrots lengthwise and then each length into 8 or 10 pieces.

Throw the carrots into the pot and cook 6 to 8 minutes. The carrots should be tender but not mushy.

Pour the carrots and water into the blender. Puree until smooth.

Pour into two ice cube trays and allow to cool.

Wrap and freeze.

chef's notes

Super-Fast Carrot Puree You know those little bags of "baby carrots" they have in the store. Everyone buys them when they decide to go on a diet! They are actually big carrots that have just been mechanically peeled and whittled down to a consistent size—which explains why they are a bit more expensive. But "expensive" is relative in the carrot world and they make this recipe SUPER FAST by eliminating almost all the prep work. So go for it.

nutrition tip
Carrots are packed with Vitamin A, which is terrific for your skin and night vision. Love that beta-carotene!

perfectly basic butternut

- **YIELD 36 OUNCES**
- **6 MONTHS PLUS**

INGREDIENTS

4 pounds butternut squash
(about 2 medium-sized
butternuts or 1 really
big one)

8 ounces water

10 ounces apple juice

Preheat oven to 400°F.

Cut the squash lengthwise. Remove seeds with a spoon.

Place squash flesh side down on a sheet tray.

Pour water onto the sheet tray.

Roast approximately 60 to 75 minutes until tender. The squash should be bubbling and caramelized.

Allow to cool 10 to 15 minutes so you can hold it without a problem.

Spoon out the flesh and pour into the blender with apple juice. Puree until smooth.

Pour into two ice cube trays and allow to cool.

Wrap and freeze.

chef's notes

Save yourself the cleanup. Parchment paper is a dishwasher's lifesaver. Use it and cleanup is easy. Forget it and you'll be scrubbing the caramelized goodness of butternut squash off every corner of the sheet tray. Another lifesaver is a Silpat. It is a silicone nonsticking baking mat. It essentially works like parchment paper but is even more nonsticking. Plus, it is reusable.

I prefer roasting squash and sweet potato. It is much better than steaming or boiling them. It is WAY better than nuking them in the microwave. The caramelization of the flesh creates a much richer and complex flavor.

Butternut squash is a nutritional all-star, one of the best vegetables you can eat. It's packed with Vitamin A and also contains Vitamin C, potassium, and dietary fiber.

perfectly basic sweet potato

- YIELD 36 OUNCES
- 6 MONTHS PLUS

INGREDIENTS

2½ pounds sweet potato
(about 2 medium-sized
potatoes or 1 really big
one)

24 ounces water

Preheat oven to 400°F.

Cut the potatoes lengthwise.

Place potatoes flesh side down on a sheet tray.

Pour 8 ounces of the water onto the sheet tray.

Roast approximately 60 minutes until tender. The potatoes should be bubbling and caramelized.

Allow to cool 10 to 15 minutes so you can hold the potatoes without a problem.

Spoon out the flesh and pour into the blender with remaining water. Puree until smooth.

Pour into two ice cube trays and allow to cool.

Wrap and freeze.

nutrition tip
Sweet potatoes are one of the best vegetables you can eat. They are loaded with carotenoids, Vitamin C, potassium, and fiber.

sweet zucchini and carrot

- YIELD APPROXIMATELY
  32 OUNCES

- 6 MONTHS PLUS

INGREDIENTS

1 pound zucchini

½ pound carrots

2 apples (about 6 ounces each)

12 ounces water

Wash zucchini. Cut each in half lengthwise and cut each length into 8 to 10 pieces.

Wash and peel carrots. Cut each in half lengthwise and cut each length into 8 to 10 pieces.

Wash apples. Peel (optional). Cut in half. Remove seeds and stems with a melon baller. Cut each half into 8 to 10 pieces.

Add carrots and water into 4-quart pot. Turn on high heat and cook 8 minutes. Stir occasionally.

Add zucchini and apples and cook additional 2 minutes.

Pour everything into the blender. Puree until smooth.

Pour into two ice cube trays and allow to cool.

Wrap and freeze.

p.e.a. (pea, edamame, and apple)

- YIELD 38 OUNCES
- 8 MONTHS PLUS

INGREDIENTS

½ pound frozen peas

½ pound frozen edamame
(soybeans)

2 apples

8 ounces apple juice

Fill a 4-quart pot halfway with water. Bring to a rolling boil over high heat.

While water is coming to a boil get your "green veggie shocking station" ready. You'll need:

- Colander

- Large bowl filled with ice and cold water. You want as much ice as possible.

Peel the apples and then remove the seeds and stems with a melon baller. Cut in half and then cut each half into sixths.

Pour the peas and edamame into the colander. Run cool water over them to get rid of any ice crystals (which will allow the boiling water to come back to a boil faster).

Pour the peas, edamame, and apple into the boiling water. Cook for 3 minutes on highest heat.

Pour peas, edamame, and apple into the colander. Run cold water over them and pour them into the ice bath. Allow to chill for 3 minutes. Pour back into the colander and pick out any remaining ice.

Pour mix in the blender and add the apple juice. Puree until smooth.

Pour into two ice cube trays.

Wrap and freeze.

continued

chef's notes

Edamame is great nutrition. That didn't impress my Henry! The first time I made this dish I used 100 percent edamame. I figured I eat them straight at the sushi restaurant down the street. But it was too much for him. He spat it up in a second. Not one of the kids ever swallowed a single bit! It was too dominant and had no sweetness. So I settled on balancing the flavor with the sweetness of pea and apple. It makes a nice combination. Plus it comes out this cool teal green color.

nutrition tip
Edamame is otherwise known as soybeans. Edamame is a complete protein packed with amino acids. It is also a great source of fiber, essential fatty acids, and isoflavones.

carrot and ginger

- YIELD 38 OUNCES
- 8 MONTHS PLUS

INGREDIENTS

1½ pounds carrots

1 tablespoon fresh ginger, minced

20 ounces water (that's 2½ cups)

Put the water into a 4-quart pot and put on high heat.

Wash and then peel the carrots.

Cut off the stems and discard.

Cut the carrots lengthwise and then cut each length into 8 or 10 pieces.

Peel the ginger and mince (see Chef's Notes).

Throw the carrot and ginger into the pot and cook 6 to 8 minutes. The carrots should be tender but not mushy.

Pour the entire contents of the pot into the blender. Puree until smooth.

Pour into two ice cube trays and allow to cool.

Wrap and freeze.

chef's notes

I cut the carrots lengthwise so there is a flat surface. That makes cutting them crosswise easier and safer. Line 4 or 5 up in a row and move through this prep work even faster.

The best way to peel ginger is with the edge of a spoon. Try it!

One of the first things a new cook does in his or her first kitchen job is peel vegetables! As a newbie I did my fair share of fifty-pound bags of carrots, potatoes, and onions. The key to mundane and repetitive prep work is to have a system. Saving five seconds per carrot when you are dealing with five hundred carrots saves over forty minutes of work. Remove all the carrots from the bag at once (instead of going in and out of the bag each time). Peel all the carrots without removing the peeler from your hand. Once they are peeled cut the ends off two at a time. Then clear your cutting board of the mess because everything

continued

moving forward is a keeper. Finally make your cuts—make your lengthwise cuts and then make your crosswise cuts four at a time. As a new cook, doing this kind of stuff fast gets you promoted. As a new parent it gets you out of the kitchen faster!

Ginger is my favorite flavor enhancer for little babies. It gives food a slightly Asian flavor and I find it very soothing on the palate. This recipe, with a little more seasoning and a garnish of crème fraîche, often makes it onto my menus.

creamy cauliflower

- YIELD APPROXIMATELY
  40 OUNCES

- 8 MONTHS PLUS

INGREDIENTS
1 head cauliflower
16 ounces whole milk

Remove the leaves and stem of the cauliflower by inserting a paring knife in the base of the vegetable and cutting out the core. The cauliflower will fall into lots of smaller pieces that you can break further by hand. Each piece should be about the size of a golf ball before it goes in a pot.

Put milk and cauliflower into a 4-quart pot and bring to a simmer over high heat.

As soon as it simmers, reduce heat to medium-low and cover.

Cook 12 to 15 minutes. (Try to avoid letting the milk boil over. It is a mess to clean up. If it begins to boil over, reduce heat further.)

Pour everything through a strainer with a bowl underneath. Reserve the liquid.

Put cauliflower in the blender with half the cooking liquid and begin to puree.

Add additional liquid as necessary.

Puree until smooth.

Pour into two ice cube trays and allow to cool.

Wrap and freeze.

chef's notes

What is cool about this dish is how similar it is in appearance to mashed potatoes. The texture is incredibly smooth and white. The dish is very creamy. Add some butter and you could fake out most people. Like mashed potatoes, this cauliflower puree is a great canvas for other flavors. You could fold in cheeses, spices, roasted garlic, or vegetable purees (see my next recipe). Curried cauliflower would make a great side dish for the adults and really adventurous one-year-olds. Try with yellow Madras curry. It is sweet and aromatic without being hot. It would be great with this puree.

get your greens, 1

- YIELD APPROXIMATELY
  40 OUNCES
- 8 MONTHS PLUS

INGREDIENTS

¼ pound spinach leaves, washed and rinsed (see Chef's Notes)

¼ pound broccoli florets and tender stems, washed (see Chef's Notes)

16 ounces water

1 head cauliflower

16 ounces milk

Put the water into a 4-quart pot and turn on high to bring to a boil.

While the water is coming to a boil prepare an ice bath and a colander.

As soon as the water is at a rolling boil add the spinach. Cook uncovered 15 to 20 seconds.

Remove the spinach with tongs and place in ice bath.

Add the broccoli florets and stems. Cook uncovered 4 minutes.

Pour the water and broccoli into the colander. Add broccoli to the ice bath.

Return pot to stove and add milk and cauliflower. Bring to a simmer over high heat.

As soon as it simmers, reduce heat to medium-low and cover.

Cook 12 to 15 minutes. (Try to avoid letting the milk boil over. It is a mess to clean up. If it begins to boil over, reduce heat further.)

While cauliflower is cooking remove spinach and broccoli. Squeeze the excess liquid out of the spinach and let the broccoli drain in the colander.

Pour cauliflower and milk through colander with a bowl underneath. Reserve the liquid.

Add cauliflower to ice bath (add more ice if needed) and let cool for 2 to 3 minutes.

Put cold cauliflower, broccoli, and spinach in the blender with half the cooking liquid and begin to puree.

Add additional liquid as necessary.

Puree until smooth.

Pour into two ice cube trays and allow to cool.

Wrap and freeze.

continued

chef's notes

Eat your broccoli . . . all of it! You can use almost the entire broccoli. Most people throw out the stem even though it is delicious. If the stem is tender use the entire thing. Simply slice it into small pieces like coins. If it is a bit woody peel the stem with a peeler, like a carrot, and then cut it into coins.

Once my kids transitioned to whole food, I found they enjoyed small florets of steamed broccoli and the stems, which I would cut like little green carrot sticks. They are good for little fingers.

Fresh fully grown spinach is nearly impossible to clean under running water. It is best to fill a large bowl or sink with cold water and submerge the spinach. Move it around rubbing the leaves with your hands to remove the sand. Remove the spinach from the water and repeat the process two more times. In culinary school we called it triple-washed spinach. The easy alternative is to use baby spinach, which is already washed and cleaned. If you use this, just wash once under running water.

There is a decent amount of fibrous roughage in this recipe. So . . . there is potential for gas. Best to introduce at lunch and not just before bedtime.

nutrition tip
Broccoli is one of the most nutrient-dense foods known. Like other cruciferous vegetables, broccoli contains phytonutrients, which have significant anti-cancer effects.

get your greens, 2

- YIELD APPROXIMATELY
  46 OUNCES

- 8 MONTHS PLUS

INGREDIENTS

¼ pound spinach leaves,
washed and rinsed

½ pound asparagus,
pencil thin and washed
(see Chef's Notes)

16 ounces water

1 head cauliflower

16 ounces milk

Put the water into a 4-quart pot and turn heat on high to bring to a boil.

While the water is coming to a boil prepare an ice bath and a colander.

As soon as the water is at a rolling boil add the spinach. Cook uncovered 15 to 20 seconds.

Remove the spinach with tongs and place in ice bath.

Cut the bottom 1 inch off the asparagus. Add the asparagus spears. Cook uncovered 2 minutes for pencil thin asparagus.

Remove the asparagus from the water with tongs and add to the ice bath.

Discard water and return pot to stove. Add milk and cauliflower. Bring to a simmer over high heat.

As soon as it simmers, reduce heat to medium-low and cover.

Cook 12 to 15 minutes. (Try to avoid letting the milk boil over. It is a mess to clean up. If it begins to boil over, reduce heat further.)

While cauliflower is cooking remove spinach and asparagus. Squeeze the excess liquid out of the spinach. Cut the asparagus into 1-inch segments.

Pour cauliflower and milk through colander with a bowl underneath. Reserve the liquid.

Add cauliflower to ice bath (add more ice if needed) and let cool for 2 to 3 minutes.

Put cold cauliflower, asparagus, and spinach in the blender with half the cooking liquid and begin to puree.

Add additional liquid as necessary.

Puree until smooth.

Pour into two ice cube trays and allow to cool.

Wrap and freeze.

continued

chef's notes

Asparagus cooking times vary based on the thickness of the stalk. I selected the pencil thin ones because they are very tender, quick cooking, and require no peeling. The downside is they can overcook in an instant. A chef friend of mine told me that Julia Child once taught her a test to determine the perfect doneness for asparagus. Simply grab the asparagus with two fingers on the lower half of the stalk. When perfectly cooked the top should bend and point to what would be 11 or 1 on a clock!

get your greens, 3

- **YIELD APPROXIMATELY 40 OUNCES**

- **8 MONTHS PLUS**

INGREDIENTS

¼ pound spinach leaves, washed and rinsed

¼ pound green beans, stems removed and washed

16 ounces water

1 head cauliflower

16 ounces milk

Put the water into a 4-quart pot and turn heat on high to bring to a boil.

While the water is coming to a boil prepare an ice bath and a colander.

As soon as the water is at a rolling boil add the spinach. Cook uncovered 15 to 20 seconds.

Remove the spinach with tongs and place in ice bath.

Add the green beans. Cook uncovered 3 minutes.

Remove the green beans from the water with tongs and add to the ice bath.

Discard water and return pot to stove. Add milk and cauliflower. Bring to a simmer over high heat.

As soon as it simmers, reduce heat to medium-low and cover.

Cook 12 to 15 minutes. (Try to avoid letting the milk boil over. It is a mess to clean up. If it begins to boil over, reduce heat further.)

While cauliflower is cooking remove spinach and green beans. Squeeze the excess liquid out of the spinach. Cut the beans into 1-inch segments.

Pour cauliflower and milk through colander with a bowl underneath. Reserve the liquid.

Add cauliflower to ice bath (add more ice if needed) and let cool for 2 to 3 minutes.

Put cold cauliflower, green beans, and spinach in the blender with half the cooking liquid and begin to puree.

Add additional liquid as necessary.

Puree until smooth.

Pour into two ice cube trays and allow to cool.

Wrap and freeze.

continued

chef's notes

All the Get Your Greens recipes use cauliflower as a base. Straight broccoli, green beans, or asparagus tend to create a really strong unpleasant flavor. The milk and the cauliflower provide a much more desirable balance.

nutrition tip

Cauliflower and other cruciferous vegetables, like broccoli and cabbage, contain compounds that may help prevent cancer. It's also packed with Vitamin C and Vitamin K.

ratatouille and polenta

- YIELD APPROXIMATELY
  1½ CUPS OF RATATOUILLE
  AND 2 CUPS OF POLENTA

- 12 MONTHS PLUS

INGREDIENTS

1 to 2 tablespoons extra
  virgin olive oil

1 cup zucchini,
  small diced

¼ cup yellow onion, small
  diced

½ cup red or yellow
  pepper, small diced

2 cloves garlic, minced

1 cup tomato, small diced

2 ounces water

3 to 4 leaves fresh basil,
  rough chopped (or ½
  teaspoon dried)

Polenta as needed (cooked)

- POLENTA

10 ounces water

¼ cup instant polenta

1 tablespoon unsalted
  butter

¼ cup grated Parmesan
  cheese

Heat oil in pan. Add zucchini, onion, and pepper. Cook 2 minutes. Stir occasionally.

Add garlic and cook 1 minute. Stir occasionally. The onion and pepper should be soft and the garlic aromatic.

Add tomato. Cook 1 minute.

Add water and bring to a simmer. Simmer for 10 minutes, adding fresh basil in final 2 minutes.

Spoon the ratatouille on top of a small bowl of warm polenta.

TO PREPARE THE POLENTA

Bring water to a boil.

Pour in polenta while whisking and allow mixture to return to a boil. Cook over medium heat for 5 minutes. The mixture will bubble and pop, so be careful. Remove from heat and fold in butter and cheese.

creamy butternut with nutmeg

- YIELD 36 OUNCES
- 10 MONTHS PLUS

INGREDIENTS

4 pounds butternut squash (about 2 medium-sized butternuts or 1 really big one)

16 ounces water

8 ounces whole milk, hot

½ teaspoon ground nutmeg

Preheat oven to 400°F.

Cut the squash lengthwise. Remove seeds with a spoon.

Place squash flesh side down on a sheet tray.

Pour water onto the sheet tray.

Roast approximately 60 to 75 minutes until tender. The squash should be bubbling and caramelized.

Allow to cool 10 to 15 minutes so you can hold it without a problem.

Spoon out the flesh and pour into the blender with hot milk and nutmeg. Puree until smooth.

Pour into two ice cube trays and allow to cool.

Wrap and freeze.

chef's notes

There are many types of hard squash available. Butternut just happens to be the most popular and the most widely available. It is also really easy to clean and remove the flesh from the skin after cooking. Feel free to use acorn squash or other hard squashes that you enjoy.

proteins, legumes, and grains

alba's chicken soup

- YIELD APPROXIMATELY 2 GALLONS

- 8 MONTHS PLUS

INGREDIENTS

6 quarts water

1 whole chicken, majority of fat removed

5 cloves garlic, minced

1 cup onion, diced (about ½ medium onion)

1 cup brown rice, uncooked

1 tomato, small diced

1 pound carrots, small diced (about 5 cups)

1 pound celery, small diced (about 4 cups)

1 potato, small diced (a small potato, about 6 to 8 ounces)

¼ pound green beans, small diced

½ pound zucchini, small diced

½ pound yellow squash, small diced

1 cup peas

5 ounces spinach, rough chopped

½ bunch cilantro, rough chopped

In an 8-quart or bigger stockpot, bring the water to a simmer. Add chicken, garlic, and onion. Simmer for 45 minutes.

Remove chicken and reserve.

Add brown rice and tomato. Simmer for 15 minutes.

During this time remove ALL the meat from the chicken and rough chop it. Be sure to remove ALL the fat and any bones or cartilage.

Add carrots, celery, and potato. Simmer for 15 minutes and stir.

Add green beans, zucchini, and yellow squash. Simmer 10 minutes and stir.

Add the peas and the roughly chopped chicken and spinach. Simmer 5 minutes and stir.

Add the cilantro and stir.

Working in batches puree the soup to desired consistency.

Pour into two ice cube trays and allow to cool.

Wrap and freeze.

chef's notes

This is the recipe our kids have thrived on for the past two years. At seven or eight months it was fully pureed. Batch by batch we pureed it less and less. They are all so happy when they have a meal of Alba's Chicken Soup. Norah loves eating it, too.

When Henry hit his anti-vegetable stage, this is how we got him his veggies.

Don't be intimidated by the size of this recipe or the extensive list of ingredients. It is a big recipe because your baby will love it and you'll only have to make it every six or eight weeks. If you omit a vegetable or two, it won't matter. If you add a little bit more of one thing and a little less of another, it won't matter.

poached salmon with carrot

- YIELD 38 OUNCES
- 8 MONTHS PLUS

INGREDIENTS

1 pound carrots, peeled

24 ounces water

1 tablespoon butter

½ cup yellow onion, small diced

½ cup celery, small diced (about ½ a celery stalk)

2 cloves garlic, smashed

½ cup zucchini, small diced (about ⅓ of a zucchini)

6 ounces fresh salmon, cut into 4 pieces

Put 20 ounces of water into a 4-quart pot and put on high heat.

Wash and then peel the carrots.

Cut off the stems and discard.

Cut the carrots lengthwise and then each length into 8 or 10 pieces.

Throw the carrots into the pot and cook 6 to 8 minutes. The carrots should be tender but not mushy. Pour the carrots into the blender.

Using the same 4-quart pot, add the butter and put on medium heat.

Once the butter melts, add the onion, celery, and garlic. Stir occasionally and cook for approximately 5 minutes. The onion should be translucent and soft.

Add the zucchini, salmon, and the remaining water. Bring the water to a simmer. Drop temperature to medium-low and cover. Cook for 6 minutes.

The fish should be just cooked through. Pour entire contents of pot onto the carrots in the blender. Add the remaining 4 ounces of water, if necessary. Puree until smooth.

chef's notes

This is an excellent introduction to fish. The baby is already comfortable with carrots and this is nothing more than aromatically poached fish and carrot puree. It is a very pretty yellow color.

poached halibut

- YIELD 38 OUNCES
- 8 MONTHS PLUS

INGREDIENTS

1 pound peas, cooked and shocked exactly like Perfectly Basic Pea on page 71

8 ounces water

1 tablespoon butter

½ cup yellow onion, small diced

½ cup celery, small diced (about ½ celery stalk)

½ cup carrot, small diced (about ½ carrot)

2 cloves garlic, smashed

½ cup zucchini, small diced (about ⅓ zucchini)

6 ounces fresh halibut, cut into 4 pieces

Puree the peas with 4 ounces of water. Reserve.

In a 4-quart pot, add the butter and put on medium heat.

Once the butter melts, add the onion, celery, carrot, and garlic. Stir occasionally and cook for approximately 5 minutes. The onion should be translucent and soft.

Add the zucchini, halibut, and remaining water. Bring the water to a simmer. Drop temperature to medium-low and cover. Cook for 6 minutes.

The fish should be just cooked through. Pour entire contents of pot onto the peas. Add the remaining 4 ounces of water if necessary. Puree until smooth.

chef's notes

Like the Poached Salmon recipe, this is an excellent introduction to fish. The baby is already comfortable with peas and this is nothing more than aromatically poached fish and pea puree.

You can substitute other whitefish in this recipe but I would seek something fairly neutral and safe. Try cod, rockfish (striped bass outside the mid-Atlantic), or tilapia.

nutrition tip

Halibut are truly delicious and nutritious. A very good source of high-quality protein, halibut are rich in significant amounts of a variety of important nutrients including the minerals selenium, magnesium, phosphorus, and potassium; the B vitamins B_{12}, niacin, and B_6; and perhaps most important, the beneficial omega-3 essential fatty acids.

slow beef stew

- YIELD 36 OUNCES
- 10 MONTHS PLUS

INGREDIENTS

2 tablespoons canola oil

2 cups yellow onion, small diced

1 cup carrot, small diced (about 1 medium carrot)

1 cup celery, small diced (about 1 stalk)

1 tomato, diced (about 1 medium tomato)

4 cloves garlic, rough chopped

8 ounces beef, boneless short rib, all excess fat removed, cut into 4 pieces

3 to 4 sprigs fresh thyme (optional)

3 to 4 bay leaves (optional)

16 ounces water

¼ cup brown rice, uncooked

8 ounces zucchini, small diced

1 cup spinach, rough chopped

¼ cup fresh parsley, rough chopped

In a 4-quart pot, add the oil and put on medium-high heat.

Add onion, carrot, and celery. Cook 3 minutes.

Add tomato, garlic, and beef. Cook 2 to 3 minutes.

Add the optional herbs and water. Bring to a simmer and reduce heat to low. Cover and simmer 20 minutes.

Add rice. Cover and simmer for 40 minutes.

Add zucchini, spinach, and parsley. Simmer an additional 5 minutes.

Pour contents into blender and puree to desired consistency.

chef's notes

We use boneless short ribs all winter at the restaurants. They are a great cut of meat from the chuck (upper rib and shoulder) for braising. And like most braising cuts of beef, they are a great value. You can substitute any cut of beef that is appropriate for braising in this recipe.

ginger beef

- YIELD 36 OUNCES
- 10 MONTHS PLUS

INGREDIENTS

2 tablespoons canola oil

2 cups yellow onion, small diced

1 cup carrot, small diced (about 1 medium carrot)

1 cup celery, small diced (about 1 stalk)

2 tablespoons fresh ginger, chopped

4 cloves garlic, rough chopped

8 ounces beef, boneless short rib, all excess fat removed, cut into 4 pieces

16 ounces water

¼ cup brown rice, uncooked

½ cup peas

1 cup spinach, rough chopped

¼ cup fresh cilantro, rough chopped

In a 4-quart pot, add the oil and put on medium-high heat.

Add onion, carrot, and celery. Cook 3 minutes.

Add ginger, garlic, and beef. Cook 2 to 3 minutes.

Add the water. Bring to a simmer and reduce heat to low. Cover and simmer 20 minutes.

Add rice. Cover and simmer for 40 minutes.

Add peas, spinach, and cilantro. Simmer an additional 5 minutes.

Pour contents into blender and puree to desired consistency.

chef's notes

This could be dinner for Mom and Dad, too. Add some heat with chopped jalapeños or Thai chiles, and some sweetness in the form of diced pineapples. Finish it all with some salt, pepper, and soy sauce. Yum, dinner is served.

ginger chicken

Just substitute 8 ounces of diced boneless skinless chicken for beef and eliminate the first 20-minute simmering period.

meatballs

- YIELD 16 MEATBALLS
- 12 MONTHS PLUS

INGREDIENTS

½ pound ground beef

½ pound ground veal

½ pound ground pork

1 egg, beaten

¼ cup bread crumbs

¼ cup yellow onion, minced

2 cloves garlic, minced

1 cup grated Parmesan cheese

¼ cup fresh parsley, chopped

2 ounces extra virgin olive oil

Using very clean hands, completely mix first nine ingredients together in a bowl.

Using an ice cream scoop, divide the mixture into 16 balls.

Using a large thick-bottomed pan (a cast-iron skillet is ideal), heat the olive oil over medium heat.

Gently place meatballs into the pan. Occasionally turn the meatballs until evenly browned and cooked through, approximately 15 to 20 minutes.

Allow to cool and then refrigerate for up to 3 days or freeze.

roasted red pepper and pomegranate hummus

- YIELD 30 OUNCES
- 10 MONTHS PLUS

INGREDIENTS

3 red peppers

2 cups chickpeas, cooked

6 ounces pomegranate
   juice

TO ROAST THE PEPPERS

On a gas range turn on three of the burners to high. Place the peppers directly on the range exposed to the open flame. Turn often with a pair of tongs and allow to char for 5 to 7 minutes. The peppers should be entirely charred black.

Place the peppers in a large bowl and cover with plastic wrap. Allow to sit for 5 minutes.

Remove the plastic wrap and place the bowl in the sink and fill with cool water. Grab the peppers and rub off the char with your hands. Remove peppers and place on a cutting board. Pour out the water in the bowl and refill with cool water. Return the peppers to the water.

Rip off the stems of the peppers and wash out the seeds. It is fine to rip the peppers in half if it is easier.

Run the peppers under cool water and place on a cutting board. Remove remaining char with a paring knife.

TO PREPARE THE CHICKPEAS

Take 1 cup of dried chickpeas and place in a bowl with about 3 cups of water (1½ quarts). Cover and allow to soak overnight.

Drain and place in pot with 3 cups of water.

Bring to a boil and then reduce heat to a simmer. Cook 2½ to 3 hours (yes, this is a pain). You'll get about 3 cups of cooked chickpeas from 1 cup of dried chickpeas.

Once you have the peppers and the chickpeas prepared, the rest is easy.

Add all the ingredients into the blender and puree 4 to 5 minutes until very smooth. Chickpeas can be gritty if undercooked and not pureed thoroughly.

Super-Fast Method You can buy canned chickpeas. It is not my first choice, but it is all right. Just pour them in a bowl and completely wash off the slimy, smelly juice they come in. You can also buy roasted peppers. They are also all right. You'll need 2 cups' worth to make this recipe.

This actually makes for a good adult veggie dip if you add some garlic, salt, and pepper.

nutrition tip
Red peppers are rich in nutrients. They are an excellent source of vitamins C and A, two very powerful antioxidants.

geoff's 20-minute pasta sauce

- YIELD 36 OUNCES
- YOU'LL GET ABOUT 10 TO 12 PASTA DINNERS FOR YOUR CHILD FROM THIS RECIPE.
- 12 MONTHS PLUS

INGREDIENTS

2 tablespoons extra virgin olive oil

1 cup yellow onion, very small diced

8 cloves garlic, smashed and chopped

28 ounces canned tomatoes, crushed

6 to 8 ounces water, as needed

5 fresh basil leaves, chiffonade

10 fresh oregano leaves, chiffonade

10 fresh parsley leaves, chiffonade

Grated Parmesan cheese, as needed

Cooked pasta (size suitable for your child's new chewing ability), as needed

Add olive oil to a 4-quart pot over medium-high heat.

Add onion and garlic. Sweat for 3 to 4 minutes, stirring often. Onion should be translucent and soft.

Add canned tomatoes. Mix together and bring to a simmer. Reduce heat until you have a slow simmer. Add water if sauce is really thick. Stir occasionally and simmer 15 minutes. Remove from heat and fold in the fresh herbs.

Toss ½ cup of this sauce with ½ cup of cooked pasta and top with Parmesan.

chef's notes

Henry, Grace, and Riley first started eating this at about ten months. We started off with orzo pasta (shaped like rice). There are numerous other small—kid-friendly—shaped pastas out there. Use any and all. Whole wheat pastas provide better nutrition. Most dry pastas are made from water and semolina flour. My real favorites are fresh pastas because they have the added nutritional and flavor benefit of eggs. They also cook in about 2 minutes.

pasta bolognese

- YIELD 42 OUNCES
- YOU'LL GET ABOUT 12 TO 15 PASTA DINNERS FOR YOUR CHILD FROM THIS RECIPE.
- 12 MONTHS PLUS

INGREDIENTS

2 tablespoons extra virgin olive oil

¼ cup celery, very small diced

¼ cup carrot, very small diced

½ cup yellow onion, very small diced

8 cloves garlic, smashed and chopped

8 ounces ground beef, lean, less than 10 percent fat

1 teaspoon tomato paste

28 ounces canned tomatoes, crushed

6 to 8 ounces water, as needed

1 teaspoon dried basil

1 teaspoon dried oregano

Grated Parmesan cheese, as needed

Cooked pasta (size suitable for your child's chewing ability), as needed

Add olive oil to a 4-quart pot over medium-high heat.

Add celery, carrot, onion, and garlic. Sweat for 3 to 4 minutes, stirring often. Onion should be translucent and soft.

Add ground beef and cook for about 3 minutes until almost cooked through. If a substantial amount of fat has come out, simply pour all the ingredients into a colander and let the fat drip away. Return ingredients to the pot and continue cooking.

Add tomato paste to the pot. Stir with a spoon so it coats all the vegetables. Cook another 2 to 3 minutes.

Add crushed tomatoes. Mix together and bring to a simmer. Reduce heat until you have a slow simmer. Add water if sauce is really thick. Stir occasionally and simmer 20 minutes.

Add basil and oregano. Simmer 5 more minutes.

Toss ½ cup of this sauce with ½ cup of cooked pasta and top with Parmesan.

chef's notes

I use imported San Marzano tomatoes. They are a bit more expensive but there is so much tomato in the can that I usually have to add some water to all my tomato sauce recipes to get the desired consistency. That improves yield and makes them ultimately less expensive. Additionally, I sometimes like to substitute ground chicken, turkey, or pork for the ground beef. Just be sure it is lean— there is no need for excess fat in this recipe.

To prepare the adult version of this dish simply add ½ teaspoon of fennel seed, 1 teaspoon of crushed red pepper, 2 teaspoons of kosher salt, and 2 teaspoons of freshly ground black pepper along with the dried oregano and basil.

When freezing this recipe, do not include the pasta.

orzo and cheese "mac 'n' cheese"

- YIELD 24 OUNCES
- 10 MONTHS PLUS

INGREDIENTS

2 ounces butter, cut into cubes

¼ cup yellow onion, very small diced

¼ cup all-purpose flour

2 cups milk, hot

½ teaspoon ground nutmeg

8 ounces mild cheddar cheese, grated

1 to 2 splashes hot sauce (seriously . . . it helps the dish but if you think it is too weird to make baby food with hot sauce you are free to omit. I like Cholula).

Orzo, cooked (or any other small pasta), as needed

In a 4-quart pot, cook butter and onion over medium heat until onion becomes soft and translucent.

Add flour and cook, while stirring, for 2 minutes.

Whisk in hot milk. Whisk well to avoid any clumping.

Bring to a boil. Milk will thicken. Whisk often to prevent any burning. Reduce heat, add nutmeg, and simmer 5 to 6 minutes. Continue to whisk to prevent burning.

Whisk in cheddar cheese. Simmer an additional 2 minutes and add hot sauce.

Keeps for up to one week in the refrigerator.

To serve, toss hot pasta and sauce together. You may need to thin sauce with a splash of water.

chef's notes

Kids are going to eat "mac 'n' cheese" a zillion times before they turn eighteen. I'd rather get them started on something that doesn't come from a little box and a bag of powder. This is really a variation of a classic roux thickened sauce called béchamel. As soon as possible add good things to this dish like diced chicken, broccoli, tomatoes, and parsley to create a nutritious balanced meal.

Parents will love this dish, too. You can toss your favorite pasta in the sauce, put it in a baking dish, sprinkle with bread crumbs and Parmesan, and bake it in the oven until golden brown. And ultimately every dad will realize that this recipe also makes for incredible nachos—just pour over chips, chili, jalapeños, sour cream, and salsa.

pasta with spinach ricotta pesto

- YIELD 16 OUNCES
- 10 MONTHS PLUS

INGREDIENTS

4 cups spinach leaves

2 cups basil leaves

1 clove garlic, chopped

½ cup fresh ricotta
  (about 4 ounces)

¼ cup grated Parmesan
  cheese

2 ounces extra virgin
  olive oil

2 ounces cold water

Any small pasta shape,
  cooked, as needed

Blanch the spinach and basil for 10 seconds and shock in ice water as explained on page 71.

Squeeze out the excess water and place spinach, basil, garlic, ricotta, Parmesan, olive oil, and water into the blender.

Puree until smooth.

Pour into ice cube trays, wrap, and freeze.

Toss hot pasta and sauce. Like the Mac 'n' Cheese recipe, feel free to add diced tomatoes and chicken to this recipe to further develop the pasta. And it is a great sauce for adults, too.

chef's notes

Cook with your kids! I did a variation of this sauce that also included arugula for forty-four first-graders. I tossed the sauce with handmade potato gnocchi. We all made the dish together and I included the kids on every step. Amazingly, forty-three of the forty-four kids ate the dish and loved it. I believe that when kids are connected to their food they are more willing to eat "green stuff."

parmesan risotto

- YIELD 14 OUNCES
- THIS RECIPE MAKES ENOUGH FOR ONE MEAL PLUS A NICE SNACK FOR MOM OR DAD.
- 10 MONTHS PLUS

INGREDIENTS

3 tablespoons butter

1 tablespoon yellow onion, minced (about the size of the rice)

½ cup Arborio rice

1½ cups water, hot

¼ cup grated Parmesan cheese

In a 4-quart pot, melt 1 tablespoon butter over medium heat.

Add onion and sweat for 2 to 3 minutes, stirring often. Onion should be translucent and soft.

Add rice and cook for 2 minutes, stirring often.

Add ½ cup of the hot water and cook for 5 to 6 minutes, stirring occasionally with a wooden spoon. Water will be almost absorbed by the rice.

Add another ½ cup of the water and cook for 5 to 6 minutes, stirring occasionally. Water will be almost absorbed by the rice.

Add remaining ½ cup of the water and cook for 5 to 6 minutes, stirring occasionally. At this point the rice will start becoming tender and will still be quite wet.

Cook and stir an additional 2 to 3 minutes until the rice becomes tender.

Remove risotto from heat and fold in remaining butter and Parmesan cheese. Stir until it is incorporated. Allow to cool and serve. The rice should be really wet and creamy. If it tightens up just stir in a bit more hot water.

chef's notes

Parmesan doesn't come in green cans! In the restaurants we only use Grana Padano or Parmigiano Reggiano. Both are aged cow's milk cheeses from Italy made in very strict ways. They are best freshly grated.

zucchini and corn risotto

- YIELD 16 OUNCES
- THIS RECIPE MAKES ENOUGH FOR ONE MEAL PLUS A NICE SNACK FOR MOM OR DAD.
- 10 MONTHS PLUS

INGREDIENTS

3 tablespoons butter

1 tablespoon yellow onion, minced (about the size of the rice)

½ cup Arborio rice

1½ cups water, hot

¼ cup fresh corn kernels (about ⅓ of a fresh cob)

¼ cup grated zucchini (about ⅓ of a zucchini)

¼ cup grated Parmesan cheese

In a 4-quart pot, melt 1 tablespoon butter over medium heat.

Add onion and cook for 2 to 3 minutes, stirring often. Onion should be translucent and soft.

Add rice and cook for 2 minutes, stirring often.

Add ½ cup of the hot water and cook for 5 to 6 minutes, stirring occasionally with a wooden spoon. Water will be almost absorbed by the rice.

Add another ½ cup of the water and cook for 5 to 6 minutes, stirring occasionally. Water will be almost absorbed by the rice.

Add remaining ½ cup of the water and cook for 5 to 6 minutes, stirring occasionally. At this point the rice will start becoming tender and will still be quite wet.

Add the corn. Cook approximately a minute and add the zucchini. Continue to stir occasionally. Cook an additional minute.

Remove risotto from heat and fold in remaining butter and Parmesan cheese. Stir until it is incorporated. Allow to cool and serve. The rice should be really wet and creamy. If it tightens up just stir in a bit more hot water.

chef's notes

This is a great summertime treat. Once you learn the basic risotto you can make infinite variations.

butternut and cranberry risotto

- YIELD 16 OUNCES
- THIS RECIPE MAKES ENOUGH FOR ONE MEAL PLUS A NICE SNACK FOR MOM OR DAD.
- 10 MONTHS PLUS

INGREDIENTS

3 tablespoons butter

1 tablespoon yellow onion, minced (about the size of the rice)

½ cup Arborio rice

1¼ cups water, hot

4 ounces Perfectly Basic Butternut puree (see page 74)

¼ cup dried cranberries, soaked in hot water for 10 minutes

¼ cup grated Parmesan cheese

In a 4-quart pot, melt 1 tablespoon butter over medium heat.

Add onion and sweat for 2 to 3 minutes, stirring often. Onion should be translucent and soft.

Add rice and cook for 2 minutes, stirring often.

Add a third of the hot water and cook for 5 to 6 minutes, stirring occasionally with a wooden spoon. Water will be almost absorbed by the rice.

Add another third of the water and cook for 5 to 6 minutes, stirring occasionally. Water will be almost absorbed by the rice.

Add remaining third of the water and the butternut squash puree. Cook for 5 to 6 minutes, stirring occasionally. At this point the rice will start becoming tender and will still be quite wet.

Cook and stir an additional 2 to 3 minutes until the rice becomes tender.

Add the cranberries.

Remove risotto from heat and fold in remaining butter and Parmesan cheese. Stir until it is incorporated. Allow to cool and serve. The rice should be really wet and creamy. If it tightens up just stir in a bit more hot water.

chef's notes

If your baby ate all the butternut squash puree and you don't want to get all the *mise en place* out to make more—simply substitute diced butternut squash that has been steamed until tender. Fold in a ¼ cup with the cranberries and increase the amount of water in the recipe to 1¼ cups.

very gouda grits

- YIELD APPROXIMATELY 2 CUPS
- 10 MONTHS PLUS

INGREDIENTS

10 ounces whole milk (1¼ cups)

¼ cup quick cooking grits

½ cup Gouda cheese, grated

1 tablespoon butter

In a 4-quart pot, bring the milk to a simmer over medium-high heat.

Add the grits and bring back to a simmer.

Whisk off and on for 5 minutes.

Add cheese and butter and cook for another minute while whisking.

chef's notes

This is essentially the exact same recipe (only smaller and without the salt) as we use in our restaurants for our Jumbo Shrimp and Very Gouda Grits. The ratio is 5 parts milk to 1 part grits. This makes them very creamy and perfect for a little one. It is a high-fat dish with plenty of calories (cheese and butter) and whole grain (corn) for energy. Using this ratio you can make larger batches if feeding the family, too. Just add sautéed shrimp, onions, sweet peppers, tomatoes, and andouille sausage.

If you use some and refrigerate the rest, you'll need to heat it back up with some additional milk to get the soft creamy consistency.

This is a nonfreezing recipe.

lentil soup

- YIELD 36 OUNCES
- 8 MONTHS PLUS

INGREDIENTS

1 tablespoon butter

½ cup celery, small diced
(about 1 stalk)

½ cup carrot, small diced
(about 1 carrot)

1 cup onion, small diced
(about ½ onion)

2 cloves garlic, chopped

½ pound French lentils

40 ounces water

In a 4-quart pot, put the butter, celery, carrot, onion, and garlic, and turn the burner on medium-high.

Cook for approximately 3 to 4 minutes, stirring occasionally, until onion becomes translucent.

Add the lentils and the water. Bring to a simmer and reduce heat to medium.

Allow to simmer for approximately 35 to 40 minutes.

Pour everything into the blender. Puree until smooth.

Pour into two ice cube trays and allow to cool.

Wrap and freeze.

chef's notes

As your child gets older, you won't even need to puree this soup. Lentil soup rocks. Every time I make it I remember how good it is and kick myself for taking it off the menu. To make this into the adult version I would add two strips of high-quality bacon, chopped up, at the very beginning and some salt and pepper right at the end. Substituting a homemade chicken stock for the water takes this dish up a notch, too. Serve it all with a hot baguette and some butter.

lentils and brown rice

c YIELD APPROXIMATELY
   3 CUPS

• 12 MONTHS PLUS

INGREDIENTS

1 tablespoon butter

¼ cup onion, finely diced

2 cloves garlic, minced

½ cup carrot, grated
   (about ½ carrot)

½ cup zucchini, grated
   (about ½ zucchini)

½ cup golden raisins

4 ounces water

1 cup French lentils,
   cooked

1 cup brown rice, cooked

• FRENCH LENTILS

½ cup French lentils

16 ounces water

• BROWN RICE

½ cup brown rice
   (a nutritious whole grain)

1 cup water

1 tablespoon butter

In a 10-inch sauté pan, add the butter and onion over high heat. Sauté for about 1 minute.

Add garlic, carrot, zucchini, and raisins. Sauté an additional 2 minutes, mixing often.

Add the water. Allow to cook additional minute.

Add the cooked lentils and rice. Mix well. Cook until the mixture is hot.

TO PREPARE THE FRENCH LENTILS

Add the lentils to a 4-quart pot. Turn burner to high and bring to a boil. Reduce temperature to a simmer and cook 35 to 40 minutes. Strain. Yield is about 1½ cups of lentils.

TO PREPARE THE BROWN RICE

Add the rice to a 4-quart pot. Turn burner to high and bring to a boil. Reduce temperature to low and cover. Cook 40 minutes. Uncover and fluff. Yield is 1½ cups of rice.

chef's notes

This is a recipe that will take your kids upwards and onwards. It has lots of textures and amazing nutrition. Together, lentils and rice are considered a complete protein with all the essential amino acids. The twins were still eating this after their second birthday and Riley is getting into it now. I really enjoy eating this too. It actually makes for a delightful side dish. And because this dish makes more than enough, you'll probably end up enjoying it, too.

whole grain blueberry pancakes with flax

- YIELD EIGHT 2-OUNCE PANCAKES

- 10 MONTHS PLUS

INGREDIENTS

- PANCAKE MIX

3 cups whole wheat flour

3 cups all-purpose flour

1½ teaspoons baking soda

1 tablespoon baking powder

1 tablespoon salt

2 tablespoons sugar

- PANCAKES

2 cups pancake mix (from above)

2 tablespoons ground flaxseed (aka flax meal)

2 eggs

1 pint buttermilk

½ stick unsalted butter, melted (that is ⅛ pound)

½ cup fresh blueberries

In a large bowl, combine the ingredients for the dry pancake mix. Store in a zipper bag or in a plastic container with a tight fitting lid.

Preheat griddle to 350°F. You can also use a large cast-iron pan or a nonstick pan. Just let it preheat for a while on medium heat—you'll have to practice a bit to achieve the correct and consistent heat. Pour the pancake mix and the flaxseed into a large bowl. Whisk eggs in a small bowl. Add buttermilk and then melted butter to the small bowl and whisk ingredients together.

Add the egg, buttermilk, and butter mixture to the pancake mix and the flaxseed.

Add blueberries. Slowly whisk together to just combine wet and dry ingredients.

You do not want the mixture to be smooth! Ladle mixture (about 2 ounces per pancake) onto the griddle and cook until golden brown. Flip and cook the other side until golden brown. This should take approximately 5 to 6 minutes.

continued

chef's notes

Pancakes will never qualify as a super nutritious food—especially topped with real maple syrup and butter the way we like 'em in our house. But I would be remiss to not include them in the book. This was the recipe I made for Norah at least three times a week during each pregnancy. Norah would eat three big pancakes! The twins started eating these at about eleven months. Henry still whines about the blueberries.

You can use frozen blueberries if you want. They'll turn the whole batter blue if you add them to the mixture. When using frozen I place them in the pancakes just after they are poured onto the griddle.

You can skip the maple syrup and the butter and top these with Very Blueberry and Apple puree (see page 56.)

nutrition tip
Flaxseeds and ground flax meal are true nutritional powerhouses. These tiny seeds have an abundance of omega-3 fatty acids and lignans. Lignans may benefit the heart and have anti-cancer properties.

norah's brain booster zucchini muffins

- YIELD 20 STANDARD MUFFINS

- 12 MONTHS PLUS

INGREDIENTS

1½ sticks butter, unsalted (6 ounces), softened

1½ cups sugar

2 eggs, beaten

1 tablespoon vanilla

1½ cups whole wheat flour

1½ cups white all-purpose flour

2 teaspoons baking soda

1 teaspoon salt

2 tablespoons ground flaxseed

1 tablespoon ground cinnamon

1 teaspoon ground nutmeg

3 cups zucchini, grated

1 cup golden raisins (optional)

Vegetable spray, as needed

Preheat oven to 350°F.

Using the whisk attachment of a food mixer, cream the butter and sugar on high speed for 2 minutes. Reduce speed and fold in eggs and then vanilla.

In a separate bowl, whisk together flours, baking soda, salt, flaxseed, cinnamon, and nutmeg.

Gradually pour the dry ingredients into the wet ingredients and slowly combine on low speed. Do not overmix.

Fold in zucchini and raisins.

Using an ice cream scoop distribute the dough evenly into muffin tins prepared with vegetable spray.

Bake until just cooked through. The total baking time is approximately 25 to 30 minutes for standard-sized muffins.

banana flax bread

- YIELD 4 SIX-INCH
  LOAF PANS

- 12 MONTHS PLUS

INGREDIENTS

2 sticks butter, unsalted
  (8 ounces), softened

½ cup sugar

4 eggs, beaten

1 tablespoon vanilla

2 cups whole wheat flour

2 cups white all-purpose
  flour

2 teaspoons baking soda

2 teaspoons salt

2 tablespoons flaxseed
  meal

6 bananas, very ripe

vegetable spray, as needed

Preheat oven to 350°F.

Using the whisk attachment of a food mixer, cream the butter and sugar on high speed for 2 minutes. Reduce speed and fold in eggs and then vanilla.

In a separate bowl, whisk together flours, baking soda, salt, and flaxseed.

Gradually pour the dry ingredients into the wet ingredients and slowly combine on low speed. Do not overmix.

Mash and fold in bananas.

Pour into loaf pans prepared with vegetable spray.

Bake until just cooked through. The total baking time is approximately 25 to 30 minutes when dealing with smaller sized loaf pans.

mom and dad eat, too!

veggie stir-fry "AKA SUNDAY NIGHT RECIPE"

• YIELD DINNER FOR 2 PLUS LEFTOVERS

INGREDIENTS

¼ cup canola oil

2 tablespoons ginger, minced

2 tablespoons garlic, minced

2 tablespoons scallions, white part, sliced

1 cup red or yellow bell peppers, 1-inch dice

1 cup red or yellow onion, 1-inch dice

1 cup carrot, sliced 1/8-inch thin on a bias

2 to 3 cups broccoli florets, blanched and shocked (see page 71)

1 cup pineapple, 1-inch dice

½ cup cashews

1 teaspoon crushed red chile peppers

½ cup hoisin sauce

½ cup sweet chile sauce

½ cup soy sauce, low sodium

Salt and pepper, as needed

3 cups brown rice, cooked (see page 115)

In a large sauté pan (a 12-inch cast-iron skillet or wok is ideal) on medium-high heat, add canola oil. Add the ginger, garlic, scallion, bell peppers, onion, and carrot.

Stir-fry until vegetables begin to soften, approximately 3 to 5 minutes.

Add broccoli, pineapple, cashews, and chile peppers. Stir-fry for approximately 2 to 3 minutes.

Add hoisin, sweet chile sauce, and soy sauce. Bring to a simmer and season as desired.

Serve vegetables on top of a bowl of hot brown rice.

chef's notes

This is my weekend recovery recipe and Norah and I dine on this often on Sunday nights. If my meals over the weekend lacked vegetables . . . this recipe is sure to make up for it. Feel free to explore other vegetables, too.

nutrition tip

For people worried about colon cancer risk, brown rice packs a double punch. It is a concentrated source of the fiber needed to minimize the amount of time cancer-causing substances spend in contact with colon cells. Plus it is a very good source of selenium, a trace mineral that has been shown to substantially reduce the risk of this type of cancer.

fish tacos "AKA MONDAY NIGHT RECIPE"

- YIELD DINNER FOR 2 PLUS LEFTOVERS

INGREDIENTS

1 pound halibut, cut into eight 2-ounce strips

2 tablespoons Fish Spice Mix

2 tablespoons canola oil

1 ear corn, kernels cut off the cob

2 tablespoons red onion, small diced

2 tablespoons red peppers, small diced

¼ cup cilantro, rough chopped

½ a lime

Salt and pepper or Fish Spice Mix, as needed

8 corn tortillas

1 cup Latin Slaw

1 cup Tomatillo Salsa

1 cup guacamole (see page 60)

- FISH SPICE MIX

1 tablespoon cumin

1 tablespoon cayenne

1 tablespoon paprika

3 tablespoons salt

2 tablespoons black pepper

- LATIN SLAW

2 cups green cabbage, thinly shredded

½ cup carrot, grated

2 tablespoons red wine vinegar

½ a lime

Salt and pepper, as needed

- TOMATILLO SALSA

4 tomatillos, husk removed and rough chopped

1/4 cup yellow onion, rough chopped

1 tablespoon jalapeño, diced

1/4 cup cilantro, rough chopped

Salt and pepper, as needed

Heat canola oil in a 12-inch cast-iron skillet or large nonstick pan on medium-high.

Place the halibut in the pan and cook for 1 to 2 minutes until the fish starts to brown.

Flip the fish over and add corn, onion, and peppers. Cook an additional 2 to 3 minutes until fish is just cooked through.

Sprinkle with cilantro and squeeze in lime juice. Season with salt and pepper or use Fish Spice Mix if you like the spice. Remove from heat.

Heat the tortillas in a pan or wrap all 8 in plastic wrap and zap in microwave for 30 to 45 seconds until hot and pliable.

Serve the fish and vegetables in the tortillas and garnish with Latin Slaw, Tomatillo Salsa, and guacamole.

TO PREPARE FISH SPICE MIX

Combine Fish Spice Mix ingredients and reserve.

TO PREPARE LATIN SLAW

Combine cabbage, carrot, and red wine vinegar in a bowl. Squeeze lime juice on and season with salt and pepper. Reserve.

TO PREPARE TOMATILLO SALSA

Puree salsa ingredients in a blender. Reserve.

pan-roasted salmon with lentils, rice, french beans, and spinach pesto "AKA TUESDAY NIGHT RECIPE"

· YIELD DINNER FOR 2 PLUS
  LEFTOVERS

INGREDIENTS

2 tablespoons canola oil

2 7- to 8-ounce portions of
salmon

1 tablespoon fennel seed,
crushed

2 cups Lentils and Brown
Rice (see page 115)

¼ cup water

¼ pound French beans,
blanched and shocked

1 tablespoon butter

3 ounces Spinach Ricotta
Pesto (see page 108)

Salt and pepper,
as needed

Preheat oven to 350°F.

Pat the fish dry with a paper towel and season both sides with salt and pepper and fennel seed.

Heat canola oil in a 12-inch cast-iron skillet or large nonstick pan on medium-high and add fish. Cook until the fish becomes golden brown, approximately 3 to 4 minutes, and flip.

Place in oven and cook an additional 3 to 6 minutes until desired temperature is reached.

Reheat the French beans and water together in a sauté pan over high heat. When the water is about to boil off, add butter and season with salt and pepper.

Serve fish on top of lentil and brown rice mixture with French beans served on the side.

Spoon spinach ricotta pesto over the fish and serve.

nutrition tip

The omega-3 fats in fish like salmon are great sources of those fatty acids needed for brain development, "brain-boosters." Wild salmon has more omega-3 fats than farm-raised salmon.

spaghetti and meatballs with ricotta and basil

"AKA WEDNESDAY NIGHT RECIPE"

- YIELD DINNER FOR 2 PLUS LEFTOVERS

INGREDIENTS

16 ounces Geoff's 20-Minute Pasta Sauce (see page 104)

8 Meatballs (see page 101)

9 ounces pasta, fresh (use spaghetti, linguine, or fettuccine)

¼ cup fresh ricotta

¼ cup grated Parmesan cheese

6 leaves basil, fresh

Salt and pepper, as needed

Heat Meatballs in sauce until hot.

Cook pasta according to instructions (fresh pasta usually takes 2 to 3 minutes).

Toss the cooked pasta in the marinara and meatballs. Season with salt and pepper as desired.

Serve in hot bowls and garnish with fresh ricotta, Parmesan, and basil leaves.

seared sea scallops with zucchini-corn risotto and balsamic drizzle "AKA THURSDAY NIGHT RECIPE"

- YIELD DINNER FOR 2 PLUS
  LEFTOVERS

INGREDIENTS

8 ounces balsamic vinegar
  (optional)

8 sea scallops, U10
  (under 10 per pound)

1 tablespoon lemon zest
  (optional)

2 tablespoons canola oil

16 ounces Zucchini and
  Corn Risotto
  (see page 110)

salt and pepper, as needed

In a small pan, bring vinegar to a boil and reduce heat to a steady simmer. Reduce 8 times until vinegar is syrupy and sweet. Remove from heat and allow to cool. This can be done in advance.

Pat the scallops dry with a paper towel and season both sides with salt and pepper and lemon zest.

Heat canola oil in sauté pan (a 12-inch cast-iron skillet or nonstick pan is ideal) on medium-high and add scallops. Cook 2 to 3 minutes until brown and flip. Cook an additional 2 minutes or until desired temperature is reached.

Serve in a hot bowl on a bed of the risotto.

Garnish by dipping a spoon into the balsamic reduction and allowing the reduction to "drizzle" off the spoon and onto the bowl, risotto, and scallops.

chef's notes

Scallops and risotto have been on my menus for more than four years. It is a top-three seller in every restaurant. It is easy to do at home. Just make sure you get dry (no liquid added) sea scallops. We request "day boat" scallops, which means the scallop boat goes out and back in the same day, resulting in scallops that haven't aged on a long multiday boat trip.

jumbo shrimp and very gouda grits

"AKA FRIDAY NIGHT RECIPE" (The last dinner recipe! Enjoy your favorite restaurant at least once a week.)

- YIELD DINNER FOR 2 PLUS
  LEFTOVERS

INGREDIENTS

2 tablespoons canola oil

12 jumbo shrimp, U12
(under 12 per pound),
peeled and deveined

1 cup andouille sausage,
small diced (about 3 to
4 ounces)

1 cup red onion, cut into
thin strips

1 cup red pepper, cut into
thin strips

1 cup yellow pepper, cut
into thin strips

1 cup grape tomatoes, cut
in half

2 tablespoons parsley,
chopped

6 ounces white wine

2 ounces butter, unsalted,
cut in cubes

2 cups Very Gouda Grits
(see page 113)

Salt and pepper, as needed

Pat the shrimp dry with a paper towel and season with salt and pepper.

Heat canola oil in sauté pan (a 12-inch cast-iron skillet or nonstick pan is ideal) on medium-high and add shrimp, sausage, and onion. Cook approximately 1 minute and add the peppers. Cook 2 to 3 minutes.

Add tomatoes and parsley. Cook until shrimp is 75 percent cooked through. Add white wine and bring to a boil. Reduce wine by about half and fold in butter. Season as desired with salt and pepper.

Serve in a hot bowl over Very Gouda Grits.

chef's notes

This is a longtime favorite dish in my restaurants. This is also the dish I prepared live on the *Today* show with Matt Lauer.

mango margarita

- YIELD 4 COCKTAILS
- 252 MONTHS PLUS

INGREDIENTS

6 ounces tequila
(use the good stuff)

2 ounces triple sec or
Cointreau

3 cups ice

2 cups mango chunks,
frozen

4 limes, juiced

2 lemons, juiced

1 orange, juiced

¼ cup sugar

Kosher salt, as needed

Add everything to the blender. Puree on high for 2 minutes or until entirely smooth. Pour into salt-rimmed glasses and garnish with a lime wedge.

chef's notes

Having babies is a dream come true but don't forget about you. Cheers and congratulations on being a great parent.

appendix

key nutrients and vitamins for baby

VITAMIN A

Foods rich in Vitamin A promote healthy eyes, skin, and teeth and boost the immune system. Vitamin A is found in beta-carotene, an orange pigment in vegetables. It is one of the antioxidant vitamins that can protect against cancer and aging.

Best sources: carrots, sweet potatoes, apricots, and liver.

VITAMIN C

Vitamin C is used to maintain immunity and may help fight colds. It also helps maintain integrity of cells, including those of bones, teeth, and gums.

Best sources: kiwis, oranges, papayas, bell peppers, broccoli, strawberries, cantaloupes, and cauliflower.

VITAMIN D

This is another one of those really important bone-building vitamins. Vitamin D helps the body absorb calcium. Early in the 20th century, scientists discovered that rickets, a childhood disease characterized by improper bone development, could be prevented with Vitamin D. That's why most cow's milk is now Vitamin D fortified. A 2009 federal study also showed that millions of American schoolchildren have dangerously low levels of Vitamin D. Exposure to sunlight—15 to 20 minutes a day—can help.

Best sources: salmon (especially sockeye), fish, yogurt, cheese, eggs, or fortified formula.

FIBER

After you finish breastfeeding or formula, feeding your baby fiber is important because it keeps your baby's bowels regular.

Best sources: grains, vegetables, and fruits.

IRON

Iron is key to healthy physical and mental development. A baby is born with a six-month supply, but then needs to be replenished with iron-rich foods, fortified formula, and supplements.

Iron deficiency is the most common nutritional deficiency in the United States, according to the American Academy of Pediatrics. Insufficient iron can slow your baby's brain and body growth, cause anemia, and even affect their intelligence. For that reason, the AAP recommends that all infant formula be iron-fortified. It's also good to start your solid food regimen with iron-fortified cereal.

bibliography

Dietz, William H., M.D., Ph.D., F.A.A.P., and Loraine Stern, M.D., F.A.A.P. *American Academy of Pediatrics Guide to Your Child's Nutrition*. New York: Villard, 1999.

Roberts, Susan B., Ph.D, and Melvin B. Heyman, M.D. *Feeding Your Child for Lifelong Health*. New York: Bantam Books, 1999.

Shelov, Steven P., M.D., M.S., F.A.A.P., and Robert E. Hannemann, M.D, F.A.A.P. *American Academy of Pediatrics: Caring for Your Baby and Young Child: Birth to Age Five*. 4th ed. New York: Bantam Books, 2005.

acknowledgments

Baby Love was a great project and many people are responsible for making it happen. First we want to thank our children. They make us better people and have filled our home with more love and chaos than we ever thought possible. A big shout-out to our editor, Alyse Diamond, and to the entire team at St. Martin's Press. You kept us on a tight schedule and we thank you for it. Thank you all for the copyediting and creative direction. You helped turn some recipes, experiences, photos, and research into a beautiful book. Thanks go to our agent, Lane Zachary, who introduced us to the wonderful world of publishing houses in a whirlwind taxicab tour of New York City. That was a truly memorable day. We want to thank photographer Timothy Devine and his team. Three straight days and more than three thousand photos were pretty intense. You have an amazing eye, and we will always cherish the photos you took of Henry, Grace, and Riley.

A big *muchas gracias* goes out to Alba Merida, our incredible nanny. You love our children as if they were your own. And they love you, too. Thank you for making and feeding them so much chicken soup. To Adam Verdugo, Norah's producer and friend at NBC News, who shares her tiny office and always provides great advice and technical savvy. To Frank Babb Randolph, who not only helped make our house a home but also became a last-minute savior by allowing us to borrow the fabrics and bowls found in so many of the photos.

We thank the Chef Geoff chef team who helped arrange for last-minute food deliveries and for putting *Baby Love* purees on our kids' menus. We also want to thank our parents for their support in this and every venture. Without their love and wisdom, where would we be? And lastly, we really should thank each other.

To Norah, without your encouragement *Baby Love* would never have been written. You are my best friend and I am your biggest fan. I love being your husband.

Love, GEOFF

And to Geoff, I'm lucky to have you as my husband and my best friend. You are the smartest, most creative, determined, and optimistic person I know. Plus, you make the most fabulous food.

Love, NORAH

index

about the authors

Chef Geoff Tracy opened his first restaurant at the age of twenty-seven. He now owns and operates five very busy restaurants in the Washington, D.C., area. Ever the entrepreneur, he plans on opening many more. Geoff is a graduate of Choate Rosemary Hall, Georgetown University, and the Culinary Institute of America. During his freshman year at Georgetown he met the woman of his dreams. Ten years later Geoff and Norah were married. (Sometimes the finest things in life take a little time!) As an active member of the Washington, D.C., community, Geoff serves as an executive on the board of Restaurant Association Metropolitan Washington. He contributes to more than 150 charities and organizations every year in the form of donations, fund-raising appearances, and even the Chef Geoff–sponsored Little League team. When he isn't meandering through the restaurants or spending time with his three little ones, Geoff enjoys skiing, golfing, swimming, cooking, and planning romantic vacations with his wife. His favorite food is pizza.

Norah O'Donnell became a correspondent for NBC News when she was twenty-five, and is now the chief Washington correspondent for NBC's twenty-four-hour cable news channel, MSNBC. In addition, Norah, an award-winning journalist, serves as a contributing correspondent for NBC's top-rated *Today Show*. She is a regular news anchor for NBC's *Weekend Today*, and has co-anchored the 9 A.M. hour of *Today*.

During her career, she has covered the Pentagon, Congress, and the White House; reported on three presidential campaigns; and traveled to every continent except Antarctica, including trips with both the president of the United States and the secretary of defense.

Norah is a graduate of Georgetown University, where she received a bachelor of arts in philosophy and a master of arts in liberal studies.

She is Chef Geoff's number-one fan and the proud mother of their three beautiful children. She is active in a number of charities, including the National Multiple Sclerosis Society, St. Jude's Children's Research Hospital, and the Children's National Medical Center.